THE HAPPY CAT HANDBOOK

THE HAPPY CAT HANDBOOK

YOUR DEFINITIVE GUIDE TO CAT AND KITTEN CARE

PIPPA MATTINSON
AND
LUCY EASTON

EBURY
PRESS

1 3 5 7 9 10 8 6 4 2

Published in 2019 by Ebury Press an imprint of Ebury Publishing,
20 Vauxhall Bridge Road,
London SW1V 2SA

Ebury Press is part of the Penguin Random House group of companies
whose addresses can be found at global.penguinrandomhouse.com

Penguin
Random House
UK

Design © Ebury Press
Copyright © Pippa Mattinson and Lucy Easton

Pippa Mattinson and Lucy Easton have asserted their right to be identified as
the author of this Work in accordance with the Copyright, Designs and Patents Act 1988

This edition published by Ebury Press in 2019

Design: Akihiro Nakayama
Picture credits:
Nick Ridley: 2, 8, 11, 15, 19, 33, 39, 45, 46, 47, 52, 60, 65, 66, 72, 74, 79, 86, 96, 97,
98, 100, 102, 112, 114, 116, 118, 121, 123, 127 (bottom), 132, 136, 138, 143, 145,
146, 152, 159, 160, 163, 165, 170, 172, 174, 175, 181, 184, 186.
Pippa Mattinson: 14, 24, 26, 27, 28, 58, 59, 68, 78, 81, 92, 115, 129, 134, 139.
Lucy Easton: 30, 32, 35, 43, 71, 111, 127 (top), 134, 149, 157, 179.

www.penguin.co.uk

A CIP catalogue record for this book is available from the British Library

ISBN 9781785039324

Printed and bound in China by C&C Offset Printing Co., Ltd

MIX
Paper from
responsible sources
FSC® C018179

Penguin Random House is committed to a sustainable future for
our business, our readers and our planet. This book is made from
Forest Stewardship Council® certified paper.

⁙ Contents

Pippa Mattinson is a zoologist and the founder of The Gundog Trust – The UK's first gundog training and welfare charity. She is a keen supporter of modern, science-based pet training methods, and is passionate about helping people to enjoy their pets. Visit her website for more information:

www.pippamattinson.com

Lucy Easton is a co-founder of the Red Cat Media online publishing company. She is passionate about improving our pets genetic health and raising awareness of conformational problems in our modern pedigree breeds.

A Psychology graduate, Lucy has written numerous articles on pet care and health and is known for her compassionate and science-based approach.

Introduction

The Happy Cat Handbook is all about making the most out of life with your cat. It is written for everyone who finds cats fascinating, and especially for anyone who is thinking about bringing a new cat into their lives.

As life-long cat owners we confess to being slightly obsessed about all things feline. We currently share our respective homes with Oscar and Billy, two young cats whose adventures are an enduring source of entertainment and inspiration. In recent years our interest has deepened. Since we launched the Happy Cat website (www.thehappycatsite.com) in 2016, we have pored over hundreds of published studies into cat genetics, physiology and health and behaviour, and immersed ourselves in everything cat. We wanted to know where cats come from, how they came to be such popular pets, what makes cats happy and how we can help them thrive in our human world.

This is a book that aims to answer all your cat questions. You'll learn how to solve common behaviour problems, how to find and choose a kitten or a rescue cat and which are the healthiest cat breeds. You'll discover where cats come from, why they purr and how they use their whiskers. And you'll learn how to teach your cat simple tricks, cure fussy eaters and care for senior cats. We look at the changing way in which cats are being kept and bred, and at their often complex relationship with humans. We investigate the best ways to avoid conflict between cats and their owners. Visiting the vet and entertaining bored kittens are also topics covered in this complete guide to our feline friends.

This book is the result of our explorations and discoveries. We're excited to share it with you and have you join us on our journey.

1

Getting ready
for your cat

1
Let's Get a Cat!

There will never be another cat quite like yours. And getting to know your cat is one of life's most precious experiences. In some respects the perfect pet, cats are both simple and complex creatures. Their needs are few but their personalities are multilayered and fascinating.

If you are ready to fill that cat-shaped hole in your life, this book will help you find and choose your new companion. And if you are already sharing your life with a cat, we'll help you get the very most out of your friendship, starting with raising a kitten, right through to enjoying your senior cat's autumn years.

To help us understand why our cats do the things they do, it helps to talk a little about where cats come from. We'll look at how cats have adapted to domesticity and how our friendship has developed, and discover what the world looks like from a cat's point of view.

Settling down

Getting a cat is often a turning point in an adult's life – a kind of halfway stage between being footloose and fancy-free and the heavy responsibilities of careers or parenthood. When you step into the world of cat ownership you will have plenty of company. The Pet Products Manufacturers Association estimates that 17 per cent of British households are home to a cat. And according to the American Pet Products Association it could be as high as 37% in the USA.

Cats are a relatively convenient pet. They need minimal training and can be left alone for several hours each day, yet they are not entirely trouble free, and do from time to time come into conflict with their human friends and neighbours. You'll find lots of great problem-solving tips in this book, but one of our main aims is to help you avoid getting into difficulties in the first place.

Where do cats come from?

The cat's evolution from solitary predator to domestic pet provides us with many clues to the roots of their temperament and behaviour, and understanding how your cat thinks and behaves is one of the keys to getting the most from your feline friend. In many ways, cats are unlike any other domestic pet. Their story is a fascinating one.

Domestic cats are descended from a species of small wildcats: *Felis sylvestris* which means 'forest wildcat'. Wildcats look very similar to domestic cats and can be found in many parts of the world. While they may look for all the world like a harmless tabby, the difference in temperament between pure wildcats and a domestic cat is profound. Modern wildcats cannot be effectively socialised, even if taken from their wildcat mother at a very young age, and can never be turned into pets. Hybrid cat temperaments may vary, and to complicate matters further there are now also new hybrid cat breeds created by crossing domestic cats with exotic wildcats, such as the African serval (*Leptailurus serval*), and we'll be looking at some of these increasingly popular hybrids as we go.

Domestic cats can be found in almost every habitable corner of our planet. But when and where did the first wildcat curl up on a human hearth and make

This tabby kitten bears more than a passing resemblance to its ancestor the forest wildcat.

friends? We have always known that cats and people go back a long way. We know, for example, that the ancient Egyptians kept domestic cats because their pets were included in the important ritual of mummification, and many have been found in burial sites. For a long time it was difficult to be sure that these cat mummies were the same species that share our homes today, but advances in DNA analysis have confirmed that the cats inhabiting the tombs of the Pharaohs were indeed domesticated cats genetically just like yours and mine. Recent evidence suggests that the domestication of the cat occurred originally in the Mediterranean, and that cats dispersed from there to Europe, Asia and Africa, arriving finally in North America with the first European settlers.

How did cats make friends with people?

It's thought that wildcats may have become interested in human settlements after we humans gave up our hunter-gatherer ways and took up farming. Rodents were drawn to the large quantities of grain we stored to keep our families fed throughout the winter months. Lots of rats and mice meant a readily available food supply for cats, and brought them into closer contact with our ancestors. While we had the benefit of the cat's rodent control skills, as cats became less shy and more tolerant of human activity they would have enjoyed access to warm dry sleeping quarters – and we all know how important those are to our cats.

Once tentative friendships were established, the sharing of food would have cemented the bond between us and laid the foundations for a permanent change in cat behaviour, which in time separated our domesticated friends from their wild ancestors.

Becoming social

Most wildcats are not social. They live much of their adult lives as solitary creatures, hunting, sleeping and eating alone. For a long time many people believed that domestic cats were solitary too. However, somewhere in our history, it's clear that cats developed a relationship with people that went beyond sharing resources. They acquired a need for social contact that enabled our two-way friendship to blossom. Cat lovers have always known, of course, that their cats love them back, and recent research suggests they are right. New studies demonstrate that despite their solitary origins, modern cats have an ability to form relationships with people, just like dogs do. This social side is not confined to their human friends, stray cats for example have been shown to form social groups, albeit loose ones. Cats can also develop affectionate bonds with dogs they live with, and may suffer from separation anxiety when parted from their loved ones.

Many people would argue that despite these changes cats are still not truly domesticated, at least not in the same way as their canine cousins. Our own relationship with cats is complex and different from the way we relate to dogs. Our friendship with dogs developed partly through a shared interest in hunting, an activity that dogs and humans enjoyed together. Like many dogs, cats also have a powerful and fundamental drive to stalk, pursue, grab and kill small prey animals and birds. But cats don't need or want human assistance or companionship in order to hunt. For a cat, hunting isn't a social activity and therefore a willingness to cooperate in order to survive isn't a part of a cat's character. Your cat is your friend from choice and not just from need.

What makes cats special?

In most modern homes in Britain, what our pet gets up to once they pass through the cat flap is a mystery. Cats have not only retained their independence but many cats today are still capable of feeding themselves if they have to. Those feline hunting skills can sometimes get cats into trouble, and a significant proportion of the human population actively dislike cats. Those of us who love them are usually prepared to forgive or overlook their predatory nature and prefer to focus on what we see as a cat's virtues. And even those who dislike cats often admit a grudging admiration for their survival skills. The cat's athletic prowess and adaptability to different human living conditions has enabled him to survive in all manner of different environments. He is as at home among the rooftops of an urban street as he is sunning himself on the branch of an old apple tree in a country garden.

How cats experience the world

A cat's need to be aloft and look down on the world from above is an intrinsic part of his nature, and all healthy cats love to climb. The domestic cat is perfectly equipped for the lifestyle of their choice. The paws of your cat with their sharp curved retractable claws are neatly designed for scaling near vertical surfaces. It never fails to impress us when we watch Oscar or

Billy leap at the side of an eight foot fence and land on the top with just a single kick off the fence panel on the way up, then walk effortlessly along the narrow top. Cats use a number of special features and abilities in order to balance along the top of a fence or branch of a tree. One such feature is the cat's incredibly sensitive feet. So Sensitive that most cats intensely dislike having their feet poked or held. Packed with nerve endings, your cat's paws can detect tiny changes in position. The tail is used for balancing too. Cats respond to movement of the surface they are walking on by rapidly moving their tail in the opposite direction. The cat's ability to climb and balance with ease enables him to include small birds as well as rodents in his meal plan, but he has other strings to his bow.

Cats cannot see in total darkness, but they can see in very low levels of light. The reflective surface in the back of their eyes helps them make the most of tiny traces of light and gives the cat's eye a ghostly glow at night. The curious slit-shaped pupil of the cat helps him to judge distance very accurately, an important attribute in a 'stalk and pounce' predator. Like many older humans, cats are quite long sighted and cannot focus on objects close to their faces, they also struggle to see objects that are moving slowly. But speed things up a little and your cat's vision will spring into action. Cats don't just 'see' with their eyes. Those pretty whiskers that frame your cat's muzzle are much more than mere decoration. Each whisker has its own unique pathway to the brain and together they help your cat to locate objects close to their face, navigate through confined spaces and move around in total darkness.

While cats are experts at finding their way around the outside world, and evading capture, they are vulnerable to traffic, and in some parts of the world to aerial predators such as large hawks. Friendly cats are particularly vulnerable to being

stolen or to attack by humans and unfriendly dogs. The popularity of valuable pedigree cats is also increasing, and cats like dogs, are more likely to be regarded as important family members than ever before. For these reasons, there are growing numbers of cats that now spend their entire lives indoors.

Even as a kitten, Billy's sensitive feet enable him to balance on a narrow edge.

The cat's elliptical pupil helps him to judge distance accurately.

Indoor cats and their needs

In the UK, full-time indoor cats are still in the minority; in the USA a recent study estimated that more than half of cats live permanently indoors. This appears to be a growing trend and one that may herald a not too distant future where most cats spend a lifetime in captivity. The change from free spirit to permanent house cat is one that has implications for our pets in ways that we don't always expect, in part because those natural feline attributes we have been exploring in this chapter don't always make for a relaxing room-mate. Fortunately there are ways to keep an indoor cat happy. If you have or are planning on having an indoor cat you'll find information to help you in Chapter 12: Indoors to Outdoors. There, we also look at the differences between cats that are still allowed to roam outdoors and those that are confined to the home to help you decide whether or not to allow your cat his freedom. There are pros and cons to either decision and your choice is likely to depend on your own circumstances.

The benefits of cat ownership

You probably don't need us to tell you that having a cat comes with benefits. Our own cats are an endless source of companionship and entertainment – even when they are waking us up at 3am because they've decided it's definitely time for a second dinner. Cats make us feel loved and useful, and for many a single person a cat is what makes their house a home. Children who grow up with cats learn to love and respect animals, and a cat can be a confidant when the grown-up world feels too much for them. Once a cat shares your life, you never feel alone again.

You may have heard that keeping a cat also has measurable physical or mental health benefits to the cat's human companion. A number of studies published in the 1990s indicated health benefits to keeping pets, from improved heart attack survival rates to decreased risks of asthma. Sadly, more recent studies have failed to replicate these kinds of results, or support the contention that pet ownership in general or cat ownership in particular can improve human health. So the jury is still out on this one, but ultimately it doesn't matter whether or not owning a cat brings health benefits, as the chances are you're not planning to bring a cat into your life to cure your arthritis or fix your migraines. The chances are that, like us, you just love cats and can't wait to bring one home!

Is now the right time?

In many ways the domestic cat has successfully straddled two worlds, that of the wild animal and that of the pampered domestic pet. They use our homes as shelter and befriend us, yet maintain an active and independent life that we know little about. Small wonder that so many of us long for the opportunity to bring one of these enigmatic creatures into our lives. With benefits come responsibilities, of course, and before you add a cat to your family you'll want to be sure you are ready for this new adventure. That's the question we'll be helping you to answer in the next chapter. Let's jump straight in and find out if you are ready for a cat!

2

Are You Ready?

Cats are fairly undemanding pets, but they do need some of your time and attention. There are also some basic financial costs involved even if your cat is given to you as a gift. Cats have character traits that sometimes bring them into conflict with their human friends. If you are ready for what lies ahead, you'll cope well with any challenges and your cat will add great joy to your life. In this chapter we'll look at some of the ways in which adopting a cat might change your life, and help you decide if this is the right moment to take the plunge and step into the world of cat ownership.

How much do cats cost?

Purchasing a pedigree cat can set you back by more than a week's salary. A local kitten of unknown ancestry can be anything from free to half the price of a pure-bred kitten, with more being asked for kittens in popular colours. But the purchase price of a pet is just the beginning. You'll need to budget for caring for your cat on a daily basis.

The first thing that tends to spring to mind is the cost of food. However, cheaper brands of commercial cat food won't make too much of a dent in the average family budget. Of course, the sky's the limit when it comes to how much you want to spend on cat accessories, furniture, bedding and so on. We'll look at those in more detail in Chapter 7: Final Preparations, but it's all pretty much optional.

By far the greatest essential expense in caring for most cats is healthcare. Simply owning a pet of any species or breed will involve medical costs. No matter how well bred or well fed your cat is, he will almost certainly need the occasional trip to the vet, and will also need protecting against parasites and disease.

Medical expenses and insurance

Veterinary treatment for cats with serious injuries or long-term medical conditions can be eye-wateringly expensive. Most cats are fairly healthy creatures, but they are also adventurous and fond of climbing. This means that they do sometimes hurt themselves. The *risk* of these potential costs leads many cat owners to purchase pet insurance, and we strongly recommend you do so. You don't want to end up in a position where you have to make a truly terrible decision because you can't afford to pay for a health issue that could otherwise have been resolved.

Be careful when purchasing pet insurance, especially for older cats that are at risk of chronic health conditions. Cheaper policies may let you down if things go wrong. You don't want to find that your insurance company won't keep paying out after the end of a year in which your cat develops a serious health condition, or that it won't cover your costs because there is a cap on payments. Read the small print and buy a policy that rolls over from one year to the next.

Neutering

A significant one-off cost to anticipate is neutering. We discuss this more fully in Chapter 18, but outdoor cats cannot be supervised so unless you are going to keep your cat indoors throughout his or her lifetime, or have your garden secured with cat-proof fencing (very expensive indeed), then you'll need to pay to have your male cat castrated or your female cat spayed. The case for neutering on a health basis isn't as cut and dried as it used to be, but free-roaming male cats with plenty of testosterone will wander great distances, and will get themselves into regular scrapes and fights which will keep your vet's wallet comfortably full – and that's if they survive the increase in road crossings essential to find the next female cat on heat. Entire male cats are also much more likely to spray in the house than neutered cats. Entire female cats will come into heat (noisily) every few weeks and have kittens several times a year, which you will have to feed and find homes for. Because of the downsides of owning an entire adult cat, male or female, we recommend you factor the cost of neutering into your budget.

Routine medical costs

Vaccinations will probably be your next biggest expense and regular annual vaccinations are absolutely essential for any cat that roams freely. Most vets recommend some vaccinations for indoor cats too, as some serious infections

Are you ready for life with a predator?

can be transmitted on shoes and clothing. Outdoor cats will also need routinely worming and treating for fleas.

In total, you are looking at spending as much again as you paid for a pure-bred kitten, in medical insurance and routine healthcare, together with the additional cost of neutering in the first year.

Life with a predator

We all know that cats are predators, but many people are taken by surprise the first time their pet brings home a live mouse and then proceeds to pursue it around their kitchen. If your cat has access to the outside world, he will hunt and kill small animals and birds. And many cats will bring their 'treasures' into the house, dead or alive.

Remember, it's not just small fluffy animals that some cats enjoy collecting. Oscar is an excellent spider assassin, which is great if you are arachnophobic but not ideal if you enjoy their eight-legged company. He has also at various points brought home a slow-worm (fortunately saved minus a tail), a goldfish (stolen we assume) and any number of slugs …

To begin with many young cats will kill their prey outright, but later they will learn that playing with the mouse first prolongs the fun. Most cat owners have to deal with an injured mouse or rat at some point, and a few people are simply not able to live with this side of the cat's personality. You need to think about this in advance, because getting angry with your cat is not going to help matters – he cannot help himself. The hunting instinct in most domestic cats is extremely strong, and while a collar with a bell on may help reduce a cat's success rate it doesn't usually avoid the problem altogether.

For some of us, it isn't just the rodents in our gardens we need to worry about. If you already have small pets in your home, you need to think about whether or not you will be able to protect them. The presence of a cat can also be frustrating when it comes to handling a hamster or pet rat for example, as you will have to remove the cat from the room before you can safely take them from the cage. Pets in outdoor runs will also need a securely fitting lid and a place to retreat to if the presence of a cat makes them anxious. All this doesn't mean it's impossible to keep both cats and other small pets in your home, but setting up some safety protocols will be an important part of preparing for your pet. We look at this in more detail in Chapter 9.

Outdoors, bird tables can be a great source of entertainment for a cat, but this is not what most of us intend! It's a good idea to relocate yours to an area likely to be inaccessible for cats, or to remove it completely.

Dealing with cat waste

Another habit that can cause conflict for keen gardeners is the cat's preference for using newly turned soil for lavatory purposes. You may need to relocate your seed beds or protect your vegetable garden in some way. Cats also have no respect for boundaries and will happily use next-door's rose beds as bathroom facilities. You might want to consider how your neighbours may react to having their flowers dug up.

Bear in mind also that, for the first couple of weeks at least, a new cat will be confined to your home and will need to use a litter box indoors for bathroom purposes. Pregnant women are advised to avoid handling cat litter box due to the small but serious risk of an infection called toxoplasmosis. The disease is carried in cat faeces and could harm an unborn baby. So if you are pregnant or think you might be, you need another family member to be willing to service the litter tray box for you.

Considering your dog

Many people bring cats into a home that already has a resident dog. Building a bond between your two housemates can be a challenge, especially if your cat is already an adult. In most cases, with careful introductions and a little time the two will come to accept one another, and some will become great friends. But there are situations where introductions can go very wrong. Some dog breeds are less likely to get along with cats than others. Sighthounds, or gaze hounds as they are also known, have been bred to chase any fast-moving object. They have the ability to reach high speeds quickly and to change direction at speed. This last factor is relevant to a potential cat owner. Sighthounds include the highly popular whippet and the greyhound, and there are other more unusual sighthound breeds including the beautiful saluki, but they all have one thing in common – they are hardwired to chase, and they are among the few breeds of dog that are capable of catching a healthy adult cat.

Many people will tell you that their whippet or their greyhound gets along fine with their cat, and it can happen – most often when the dog and cat have been raised together from puppy and kittenhood. But you need to be aware of the potential for disaster. It is specifically a fast-moving object that triggers the chase response in dogs inclined that way, and a cat walking around your home may not be sufficient to set the dog into action. The fact that the two get along fine in the house may not protect your cat once he is allowed out into the garden.

Sighthounds are not the only dogs that may pose a threat to a cat, some older dogs just don't like cats and are not amenable to having their minds changed. If you own such a dog you are probably aware of the potential for conflict already, but it pays to think this through before making your final decision.

Cats and your home

With the best will in the world, life with a living, breathing animal in your home is never going to be quite the same as it was before. Your home will never be quite as pristine. All cats may vomit occasionally, either from hairballs or some minor infection, and won't be able to control where this event takes place. Pippa has claw marks in her favourite leather sofa from where Billy used to race up the sides when he was small, and her previous cat Gadget regularly brought up hairballs in her bedroom. Cats shed a surprising amount of loose hair, and both Oscar and Billy leave a nice nest of fur on any chair or bed that they sleep on or lean against regularly. If you are house proud this is something to consider. But on the whole a cat shouldn't have too much impact on the structure or fabric of your home.

Do you have time for a cat?

Unlike dogs, cats don't need masses of human interaction, regular accompanied walks or daily training sessions. With a few provisos, you can still have a cat if you are out at work during the day. However, cats do need company on a daily basis in order for a bond to form between you. They also need a responsible adult to feed them at least once a day (more frequently is better) and to 'check in' with, so you'll need a support system in place for when you go away – a helpful friend or neighbour will enable you to take the occasional trip away. You can buy automatic feeders, but supervision is important because all cats can fall sick, and outdoor cats can be injured in fights or traffic accidents. Someone needs to be on hand to take swift action if a cat returns home needing veterinary attention.

If you are still at the globe-trotting stage in your life and are often away from home, it might be better to wait until your lifestyle is more settled. As we have seen, modern cats are social and return home for your company, not just for supper. An outdoor cat may wander off in your absence, even if food is regularly put down. Not only is a cat at risk if you are hardly ever home, the chances are high that he will eventually move in with someone else. Most cats are happiest if there is someone at home each evening and night on a regular basis. If you are out at work during the day but home most evenings and weekends, your cat will probably be happy to sleep away your working hours or spend them visiting neighbourhood friends.

Everything we have discussed applies to adult cats and most of it applies to kittens too. But it's a good idea at this point to mention the special needs of a kitten, because there is a little more involvement needed on your part if you bring home a kitten rather than adopt an adult cat. Most kittens are adopted at eight to twelve weeks old, becoming adults around six months later. So a kitten is essentially a six-month project that requires some extra input from you. In order for you to be aware of what you are letting yourself in for during that period, we've devoted the following chapter to kitten development.

Bring it on!

Bringing home a kitten or adult cat is of course a serious commitment. It's a responsibility that may be yours for up to 20 years. Hopefully you now have a better idea of what you are letting yourself in for! Generally, cats are not high-maintenance pets, but there is a cost involved, both financially and in terms of your time and effort, and it's important that you are ready for it.

A cat will change your life and bring some challenges, but it will also bring great pleasure. If pet insurance and cat food are within your grasp, and if you are as passionate about cats as we are, you've probably already resigned yourself to the wilder side of their personality, and are ready to take the plunge!

3

Kittens and Kitten Care

Kittens are enormous fun but they do require a little more time and attention than a grown-up cat. Both Oscar and Billy were eight weeks old when they scampered into our lives, although many pedigree cat breeders will not release their kittens until they are twelve weeks old. We'll be looking at cat breeders, home-bred kittens and cat rescues in more detail in Chapter 6: Choosing a Cat. In this chapter we focus mainly on kitten development, from the point at which you bring your kitten home until your kitten is about six months old. We want to give you an idea of what to expect at each stage, so you can decide whether you have the time and energy right now for raising a kitten.

Two-month-old kittens

Kittens at eight weeks old are very tiny indeed. Being so small makes new kittens vulnerable, especially for the first few days. Most people don't let kittens outdoors unattended until they are around six months old, but even in the house there can be risks. Billy's family worried a great deal about stepping on him to begin with, and that's with only careful adults in the house. If you have young lively children at home, it might be better to wait another week or two before collecting your little one. In either case you'll need to make a rule that everyone walks slowly around the kitten and is especially careful when going up and down stairs. Most kittens seem to be on a mission to trip someone up!

Looking after an eight-week-old kitten isn't complicated, but there are a couple of important things for you to focus on. One is keeping your kitten safe and the other is teaching him to be clean in the house. Fortunately there is a way to ensure both your kitten's safety and a great start to toilet training, and that is with the use of a designated 'safe room' for the first few

Billy at eight weeks old.

weeks. We'll talk about the safe room in a bit more detail in Chapter 7: Final Preparations but it's essentially a place where your kitten is confined for the first week or two complete with a litter box and everything else that they need. Billy's safe room was the office in Pippa's home where we work during the day. But any room where the kitten can enjoy getting to know the family, while in close proximity to a litter box and with no direct access to the outdoors, is fine.

Kittens spend a lot of time asleep and most prefer to rest somewhere cosy and raised up above the ground. Billy liked his cat caves. Pippa placed one on her desk and another on the kitchen bench. Oscar preferred to sleep at the top of the stairs. Even an eight-week-old kitten is capable of jumping many times their own body height and will soon be exploring the furniture. When they are awake, eight-week-old kittens are very playful and great fun to watch. Preferred toys are tiny light balls designed for kittens and empty cardboard boxes with holes cut in the sides. Billy loved large springs – you can buy these in packs, though watch out for them jamming the vacuum cleaner! Oscar's favourite was pieces of string with feathers tied on the end and a collection of teeny-tiny toy mice.

Eight-week-old kittens usually weigh around one kilogram (two pounds) and if well fed will put on another pound over the next four weeks. Kittens do best if fed on food specifically designed to meet their needs. There's evidence that wet food is better for their health (see Chapter 10: Feeding your Cat) and your eight-week-old kitten will need four meals a day for the next month. You'll need to space those meals out so that he is being fed every four to five hours – you can't just leave a day's food down for a kitten as they will eat it all at once and probably give themselves diarrhoea. Eight-week kittens need to visit the vet and be given their first vaccinations within the first few days at home. You'll be able to chat to your vet about any concerns you have over your kitten's food and his feeding schedule, and your kitten will be weighed and examined to make sure that he is healthy and growing well. If your kitten gets sick, you'll need to give your vet a call without delay, but with luck those first four weeks will fly past without any problems.

Three-month-old kittens

Your kitten will now be substantially more sturdy and confident than at eight weeks old. Most kittens this age will be exploring the rest of their home – and finding new ways to trip you up, so you will still need to be very careful. The safe room may no longer be necessary, though many kittens will benefit from spending their nights there for a while.

Billy was very playful at three months old.

By 12 weeks a kitten should be coming to his name, and if he isn't it is time to start purposefully training him. Don't fall for the myth that cats can't be trained, it isn't true. You'll find lots of training tips and advice in Chapter 13: Training and Tricks. It helps if you are around a great deal at this stage to teach him his name and reward your kitten frequently. A good recall might not matter now, but if you let your cat outdoors when he is older, being able to call him in whenever you want to will bring great peace of mind and help ensure his safety. Going outdoors is a great way to burn off excess energy but it's too early for that yet, so your kitten will need to play and exercise indoors.

The average three-month-old kitten weighs around 1.4 kilograms (3 pounds) – though you'll need to make adjustments to your expectation for larger breeds such as the Maine Coon. A good quality kitten food is still important and at 12 weeks Billy was munching his way through about 220 grams (7¾ ounces) of wet food each day. A large breed kitten might need half as much again, but your vet or breeder will be able to advise you if you are concerned. Most kittens this age can now cope with larger quantities of food in each meal without getting an upset stomach, and can drop down to three meals a day. During this week or the next one your kitten will need another visit to the vets for their second shots, and again this is a good opportunity for your vet to reassure you that your kitten is growing well and to answer any questions you may have. Billy was very playful at three months old. This is a peak age for wild play and you'll need to take precautions against getting scratched by those needle-sharp claws.

Biting and aggression

Biting is a normal part of play for kittens, and this behaviour does improve as they grow. While your kitten is small they will have periods of time when they are bursting with energy and very playful. It's not helpful to punish a kitten for biting, and punishment can cause even more problem behaviours. Instead, avoid interacting with your kitten when they are very overexcited. Stop the game and walk away. It's important to keep your hands well away from a kitten's teeth and paws when they are in play mode as they cannot control their reactions. This is where toys on a string come in handy.

The next few months will bring some changes in temperament, and most kittens will become increasingly active and excited for short periods of time each day as they practise their hunting and predatory behaviours. Many young cat owners will know this as a kitten's 'crazy time' and it is often a trigger for a cat to be allowed to go outdoors. There are some other factors to take into consideration and we look at that in Chapter 12: Indoors to Outdoors.

Six-month-old kittens

As you give your kitten more freedom, remember to continue to make sure that their litter box is easily accessible. Good toilet training habits at this age will last a lifetime and it's well worth going to considerable lengths to ensure that kittens are always able to get at their litter box quickly. Putting additional litter boxes in different parts of your home is a sensible precaution and you'll find lots more tips on this topic in Chapter 11: Clean and Dry.

Billy having a rest after playing with his mouse toy.

Another problem that can arise as kittens are allowed the freedom of the house is scratching. Kittens and older cats can cause expensive damage to furniture and carpets if not provided with an appropriate place to stretch their paws and claws. Again, building good habits at this stage will prevent problems in the future, and the solution is to put plenty of scratching posts in different parts of your home. These really do help prevent cats from damaging the furniture. Billy stopped using most of his scratchers once he was allowed outdoors. He only has one scratcher in the hall now, but he uses it nearly every day.

Some females will become sexually mature by six months old and will have their first season any time soon. By six months of age many kittens will have been neutered and this is usually best done before letting your cat free to roam outdoors. Your kitten will now look very much like an adult cat, and will only have a little more growing to do. The average six-month-old will weigh around 2.75 kilograms (6 pounds) and kittens this age can manage on two meals a day, morning and evening, though we recommend more frequent feeding where possible. Caring for a kitten at this stage is increasingly like caring for an adult cat, and the bulk of your work in raising your kitten to be a happy, clean, confident member of the family will soon be done!

Whether or not the four-month-kitten adventure we have just described will fit into your life depends a great deal on your working hours and on the ages of any children you have.

At six months old Billy takes up a lot more space on the desk.

Kittens and babies

Even the nicest cat in the world can accidentally hurt a baby, and older babies grabbing handfuls of fur is more than many adult cats can tolerate. If you have a baby then you need to be extra vigilant with any cat around. Kittens and babies don't understand each other at all, and are more likely to end up hurting one another than spreading joy around the family. Adult cats tend to be more mellow, which is a great thing when you've got a six-week-old baby and are not getting much sleep.

We should mention, of course, that it is never sensible to let a cat of any age sleep in a baby's room in case they go to sleep on the baby's face.

Another thing you need to consider when combining cats and babies is that kittens need considerably more maintenance than an adult cat. As we've discussed above, their meals are more frequent, they are more playful and they also get in the way a lot more! No matter how hard you try it's only natural that your baby will come first, and not only will the kitten not get as much attention as he needs, you'll miss out on a fun time. Kittens are kittens for just a few short weeks and you will get a lot more out of the experience of raising a kitten if you are not exhausted and sleep deprived.

Kittens and older kids

Older kids are a different matter and kittens can be amazing pets for children. Kittens are likely to forget to retract their claws or to have a go at chewing something inappropriate, so they are perhaps best suited for over-fives, who can be taught how to avoid getting bitten and scratched. Playing with cats and kittens is always fun for kids, but should only be done with long toys to avoid accidental injuries from claws or teeth.

Oscar arrived home a good two years before his human sister was born, so he was in the sensible adult cat phase. Or as sensible as he is likely to get! He also has a fabulous temperament and considers himself to be best friends with the whole world.

As a precaution, children who meet Oscar are taught to watch his tail and to immediately remove their hands when it twitches. Oscar has lots of child visitors and with careful supervision they have all stayed safe and enjoyed interacting with a particularly chilled-out feline.

Oscar gets on well with children.

Kitten versus cat?

Kittens aren't just super cute balls of fluff. They are balls of fluff with sharp teeth, pin-like nails and the energy of an Olympic sprinter who has been stuck indoors all week. Although the hours they spend curled up in an impossibly tiny ball in your lap are amazing, when they are awake they are pretty full on – which is great fun when you are in the mood, but trying to get dressed with a kitten hanging off your dressing gown cord and wrapping themselves around your ankles isn't easy.

Raising a kitten is a fantastic experience but the timing needs to be right in order to really make the most of it. As we have seen, young kittens need feeding more frequently than older cats and benefit from having an adult human around at regular intervals throughout the day. So while raising a kitten if you work full time is possible, it isn't ideal. Kittens are not always the best playmate for small children, so if yours are under five you might want to wait a while.

If now is not the right time to bring a kitten into your life, you might still be able to share your life with a cat. Adopting an adult rescue cat can be deeply fulfilling and enjoyable experience, and caring for an adult cat is the topic of our next chapter.

4

What Do Cats Need?

Most cats have a pretty good idea what they expect from people: free food, a warm place to sleep and absolutely no rules! People, on the other hand, are often not quite sure what to expect from a cat, or what their cat needs in return. In this chapter, we are going to investigate what's involved in living with an adult cat. It should give you an idea of what you need to provide to keep your cat happy, and how becoming a cat owner will affect your life. We'll look at how you might need to adapt your routines and your home. And we'll tease out some of the key responsibilities that cat owners face, such as providing proper medical care and an adequate diet. Let's make a start with the inside of your home.

A cat-friendly home

It's perfectly possible to bring a cat into your home without making any changes at all to the interior of your home. However, there are lots of ways to make your house more cat friendly.

Some kind of scratching surface for your cat is a very good idea, to avoid them damaging your furniture. Because cats love to climb and prefer to view the world from above, you might want to consider purchasing a cat tree or shelf for your cat to sleep on. These often come with a scratching post incorporated into the design. You should also think about removing your bone china antiques from the top of the sideboard. Most cats are not particularly clumsy but accidents can happen, and in the early days your cat will want to explore every inch of your home and won't care whether or not your household insurance covers your family heirlooms.

Adult cats don't mind being alone for a few hours, so your cat won't suffer or be lonely while you are busy working to pay for his premium treats. In fact most cats sleep for much of the day. However, while cats are awake they can and do sometimes get up to mischief. If you are used to leaving the breakfast leftovers on the kitchen table to deal with when you get home,

Most adult cats won't mind if you are out at work for a few hours.

you might want to rethink that habit. Your kitchen table is a mere hop for a cat, and the same applies to your worktop, hob and sink. Most cats can jump up to two metres from a standing start, and that is when the side of the obstacle is smooth. If there is anything to grip on to, your cat will make Spiderman look like an amateur. The best way to prevent counter hopping and stealing, is to keep worksurfaces clear of food so that there is never any reward for the cat who explores them. If you think cat paws are clean and you don't mind your cat walking on surfaces where you eat, bear in mind that cats bury their poop with their paws.

A safe environment

With an inquisitive pet loose in the house, you'll need to remember to put household cleaners away, store your medicines safely and remove anything else that might be toxic to cats, including some quite common human foods and household plants. This is not an exhaustive list, but it's worth bearing in mind that the following are all poisonous to cats:

- Onions, garlic and chives
- Coffee

- Alcohol

- Raisins and grapes

- Many human medicines

- Many flea treatments designed for dogs

- Lilies, tulips, mistletoe and poinsettia

- Some brands of chewing gum, peanut butter and other foods that have been sweetened with xylitol.

Onions are a big no-no for cats and quite a small quantity can be fatal. Because onion is such a common ingredient in many human foods this is a good reason not to share prepared human foods with a cat. Non-food items can be harmful too. Many dog flea treatments contain the chemical permethrin. Cats are extremely sensitive to this and a number of other common pesticides, so always read the instructions very carefully, don't let your cat share a bed with a dog that has just been flea treated and make sure any pest control contractor coming to your home knows you have a cat. There are other household substances that can harm pets so the basic rule for both cat and dog owners is to tidy surfaces accessible to pets before leaving the house.

Nowhere is out of bounds to a home alone cat.

A cat-friendly vet

Even if your cat is sensible enough not to swallow a battery or drink from the bucket of detergent you left standing in the bathroom, he may still get sick from time to time. One of your first tasks when bringing home a cat is to take responsibility for your new friend's health and medical care. That means finding a veterinary surgeon to carry out routine and emergency treatments, and making sure that you have a basic understanding of how to keep a cat in good general health.

Most towns and large villages have at least one veterinary practice, where there may be several vets with good coverage around the clock. You may be lucky enough to find a 'travelling' vet who offers reasonably priced home visits. This can be a real bonus for cat owners, because most cats find car travel and being taken into a vet's surgery extremely stressful.

If you can, it is a good idea to find a vet who specialises in cats and a practice that has a 'cat-friendly protocol'. Studies have shown that stress can exacerbate health problems in cats and may even predispose cats to new health issues, but there is quite a lot that can be done to reduce the impact of veterinary visits on your cat. A vet specialising in cats will use feline-friendly handling techniques – gone are the days of forced restraint. Some will also have a dedicated 'cat' examination room where dogs are not allowed.

If your vet's waiting room is mixed, with cats and dogs all in together, try to ensure your cat carrier is well out of the way of lolling tongues and enthusiastic doggy greetings. It will help your cat to feel more secure if you push the door up against a wall or cover the crate with a large blanket. If it's not an emergency, asking for the first appointment of the day can help to avoid sharing the waiting room with dogs.

Regular vaccinations

One of the first treatments your cat or kitten will be offered by your vet is a programme of vaccinations. There are a handful of serious diseases that most cats are routinely vaccinated against. They vary from country to country, and in some cases from region to region. Some states in the USA require vaccinations for Rabies for example, while others do not. New diseases spring up from time to time so it is very important to discuss what is needed locally with your own vet. It may also depend partly on whether or not your cat is allowed outdoors

Cats Protection, the UK's largest cat charity, recommends that all cats are vaccinated against feline infectious enteritis (FIE) and against cat 'flu'. They recommend an additional vaccination against feline leukaemia virus (FeLV) for any cat that is going to be allowed outdoors. However, we understand that many people are concerned about vaccine safety and it's important with FeLV to weigh up the risks as well as the benefits. No vaccine is 100 per cent safe. Occasionally a cat will have a bad reaction to a vaccine or develop skin problems at the vaccination site. These risks are rare, but as the diseases themselves recede into the past for many of us the risks of the vaccines can become a source of concern.

An American study found that five cats in every thousand had an adverse reaction in the 30 days following vaccination. Most reactions are mild and involve the cat becoming lethargic for a while, with or without a fever. We've noticed that both Oscar and Billy seem mildly unwell and sleepy for a few hours after vaccination. There is also a small risk in cats of a tumour developing at the vaccination site – this is more serious but very rare, and occurs in less than one in every ten thousand cats.

It's important to remember that vaccines have virtually eradicated some horrible diseases that killed many healthy young pets just a few decades ago, and they have greatly reduced the incidence of many other very serious diseases. Some of those diseases are still alive and kicking on a street near you, and it's those diseases that your vet will want particularly to protect your pet against. If you decide to keep your cat indoors you may feel that vaccinations are not necessary, but most medical professionals disagree as some of the diseases that kill unvaccinated cats can be carried in on shoes and clothing.

Once your cat has settled in, unless he is unlucky enough to be injured or get sick, you will hopefully only see your vet once a year for annual boosters.

Oscar sometimes feels a little under the weather after a vaccination.

Treating for parasites

There are a few routine healthcare procedures that can usually be applied at home. The most important of these are medications to keep cats free from parasites.

There are two main types of parasite that cause problems in cats – fleas and worms. Fortunately, it's fairly easy to stay on top of them if you don't let these uninvited guests get their feet under the table.

Cat fleas are a really common problem, and they don't limit themselves to biting cats. Once they are in your home they can set up shop on any number of your pets and will happily bite humans too. Fleas are not restricted to fur. They hang out in the edges of carpets around your living room, hide in cracks in the floorboards or tuck themselves down the side of the sofa. Flea bites, although not dangerous in and of themselves, are a massive nuisance and can cause intense irritation and even a nasty inflamed blister on each bite site. Fleas can be really hard to eradicate from your home, and the way to avoid a flea problem is to treat your cats regularly and *before* things get out of control.

The other main parasite your cat will need protection from is intestinal worms – tapeworms and roundworms. You'll need to routinely worm your cat, especially if they are allowed to hunt outdoors. Interestingly, tapeworms can also be passed on by fleas.

A cat-friendly diet and regular meals

Adult cats can be fed once or twice each day, so it's a simple matter to fit this into your working day. The vast majority of us feed our cats on a commercial diet designed to meet a cat's nutritional needs in a convenient package. If you can feed more often that's a bonus, as it may help to keep a cat close to home.

Though many cats move into a home with a resident dog, they can't share the same food. Dogs are able to live on a much more varied diet and most dog food contains quite large quantities of cereal and/or vegetables. Adult cats, on the other hand, need a higher proportion of dietary protein than dogs, so it's important to buy food specifically designed for cats.

Feeding a cat on commercial food is relatively straightforward, but cats do have a few quirks when it comes to food and feeding which should be taken into account. They need some variation in their diet, for example, so as not to become bored and start to refuse their meals. We will look at all of the options in more detail in Chapter 10: Feeding Your Cat.

Entertainment and company

While some adult cats enjoy playing with toys, especially if the game is spiced up with some catnip, they may need encouragement from a human playmate. You don't need to buy toys if you don't want to – you can easily make a 'hunt and grab' game out of some scrunched-up paper and string. We look at entertaining your cat in more detail in Chapter 14: Bonding and Behaviour.

Most cats don't need a lot of entertaining, but some do become lonely if left on their own for long periods. Although it's usually fine to have an adult cat if you are out at work during the day and home each evening and at weekends, there are exceptions. What doesn't work so well for many cats is an owner who is away for long periods of time. Making arrangements for a neighbour to come in and feed your cat may not be enough to keep a cat that has access to outdoors from straying further and further from home.

What cats need – in a nutshell

We hope by this point you have a pretty good idea of what's involved in caring for an adult cat. We think you'll agree that it isn't too complicated. Owning a cat will change your life a little, but none of a cat's needs are particularly difficult to meet. Routine worming and flea control together with an annual vet check and vaccinations, and a decent diet, form the basics. Splitting your cat's daily meals into several small portions will suit most cats very well – and help keep them closer to home, as will regular spells of your company. Cats are independent and don't mind spending time alone, but remember - if you are hardly ever there, leaving home is an option most cats will consider.

5

Different Types of Cat

Now you are armed with everything you need to know about basic kitten and cat care, it's time to decide exactly what type of cat you want to bring into your life.

No two cats are exactly the same. Cats come in a wonderful range of coat colours and patterns. Some, like the popular tabby, are common and easy to find. Others are confined to expensive pedigree breeds. Different types of fur and body shape are also available. You can even buy pet cats that have some genuinely wild genes flowing through their veins. These are the hybrid cat breeds, a cross between a domestic cat and a different species of cat altogether.

Exotic and pure-bred cats were fairly unusual family pets until a couple of decades ago, and apart from the Siamese and Persian breeds were largely confined to breeding enthusiasts and exhibitors. That is changing now, but before you take the plunge into the world of unusual or rare cats, it's important to learn a bit about them.

Our main concern in this section is to highlight any special requirements that different types of cat may have. We'll focus on features that can affect their health and therefore indirectly your own lifestyle and happiness. We'll also look at any special treatment that some cat coat types need, and at how friendly and easy to manage different breeds of cat are.

Cat coat colour

Some people just love ginger cats, others not so much. Some favour the black and white variety, others prefer a cat in a solid colour. Whether you are choosing a kitten or rescuing an older cat, you'll probably have heard that cat personalities may vary according to their coat colour. A fascinating study published in 2012 showed that many cat owners associate friendliness with the orange or ginger cat, whereas white or tri-colour coats were associated with aloofness. However, the

Deafness associated with white cats is less likely when their eyes are green rather than blue.

evidence to support the contention that coat colour is linked to personality is weak at best, so don't let those rumours stand in your way.

There is however one particular coat colour that we would caution against, and it has nothing to do with personality. In many mammal species there is a strong link between white fur and impaired hearing, and cats are no exception.

This link does not affect every white cat but it's important to understand the risks. Especially if you intend to let your cat outdoors, because a deaf cat is more vulnerable to traffic and predation.

It's important to emphasise that not all white cats are deaf, but the risk is significant. Among white cats in the general pet-owning population a study of 84 pure-bred cats found that 20 per cent were deaf, and just over half of those were deaf in both ears. The risk of hearing loss in a white cat is increased if the cat also has blue eyes, though a small proportion of blue-eyed white cats will have normal hearing. In some cats you sometimes get the unusual situation where one eye is blue (the eye next to the deaf ear) and the other eye is a strikingly different colour. There is currently no practical way to cure deafness of this nature in cats, and you may want to consider this risk before choosing a white kitten.

Long-haired vs short-haired cats

Both long and short-haired cats have their fans. If you are torn between the two, it's worth bearing in mind that longer coats are definitely higher maintenance. The most common issue with long-haired cats is the risk of matted fur and the need for grooming. Long hair may also increase the risk of your cat regularly vomiting up hairballs. While hairballs are often more of a nuisance to those living alongside a cat than they are to the cat, they can occasionally cause a potentially fatal intestinal blockage. To help those with affected cats we look at the topic of hairballs in more detail in Chapter 17: Horrible Hairballs and Other Furry Facts

Short-coated cats require very little in the way of grooming from their owners, though grooming does help to reduce the amount of hair floating around your house.

'Hypoallergenic cats'

If the merest whiff of a cat has you reaching for the tissues, you may be wondering whether or not to try your luck with a hypoallergenic cat breed. The idea of hypoallergenic pets was popularised in the 1980s, when an Australian guide dog breed manager attempted to create a new guide dog that could live with a blind person with a dog allergy. The experiment gave us the popular labradoodle and taught us a lot about fur and fur allergies. (Unfortunately, it wasn't a huge success from a guide dog point of view.) Since then more studies have been carried out in the quest to find hypoallergenic cats and dogs, and what follows is what we now know.

People who are allergic to cats or dogs are not allergic to their hair. They are allergic to a protein molecule called Fel d 1. All cats carry this molecule in their saliva and transfer it to their fur during grooming. It's present in the dead skin cells (dander) that cats shed each day, so a hairless cat is no guarantee of a sneeze-free zone. Cats that produce less Fel d 1, such as the Balinese and Siberian breeds, may be tolerated by some people that are sensitive to cats. A good specialist pedigree cat breeder will be able to verify the level of Fel d 1 in their cats.

However, the only way to know whether or not you would be affected would be to spend time with such a cat. And for someone with a serious cat allergy there really is no safe level of exposure to cats; there is no truly hypoallergenic cat.

Low-shedding cats

There are, however, *some* types of fur that are associated with reduced levels of shedding and these cats may be a better fit for a mildly sensitive person. Curly or crinkly fur tends to trap loose dead hair and dander – that's why poodles were chosen for the guide dog experiment and why some people who are allergic to most dogs can tolerate being in a room with a poodle. The same logic applies to crinkly cat fur, and some sensitive people find that they are able to live with a rex breed of cat.

There are some downsides to life with a curly coated cat that we need to consider. For instance, the Cornish and Devon Rex cats offer a pet with an unusual wavy or crinkly coat, but these distinctive looks come with some associated health problems. The rex coat isn't properly weatherproof either, so this type of fur isn't a great idea if you want your cat to be able to go outside.

Hairless cats

Perhaps you are part of the growing fanbase that finds cats with no hair at all more appealing. The most well-known hairless breed is the Sphynx cat. They certainly have an exotic appeal. Unfortunately the gene for baldness in cats causes some nasty diseases. The lack of coat also makes the Sphynx very vulnerable to cold or wet weather, not to mention little cuts and scrapes that would normally be prevented by the protection of fur. So this is really an indoor-only breed. We strongly recommend you read Chapter 21: Pedigree Cats before you dip into your wallet for one of these.

Miniature cats

What could be cuter? A cat just like any other, but in a tinier, more adorable package? It seems that many of us think so because teacup or miniature cats are currently growing in popularity. But this trend is causing ripples of concern among cat experts and veterinarians around the world, and it is important to understand what is involved in miniaturising a cat, and the impact of this process in terms of health and lifestyle.

In principle, there are two ways to make cats smaller. One is by breeding from the smallest cat in each litter over several generations – the cats that are miniaturised in this way are sometimes referred to as teacup cats. Normal growth and size is often an indicator of good general health, so a policy of breeding from 'the runt' of every litter is likely to result in kittens that are as sickly as they are appealing.

The other method is to breed from cats that have a genetic defect that causes a form of dwarfism, which results in the animal having disproportionately short legs. A breed of cat called the Munchkin has been created this way. Disorders responsible for stumpy legs are associated with pain and discomfort in many animals. They also interfere with a cat's ability to run, jump, eat and play.

We urge caution to anyone considering purchasing a miniature cat.

Flat-faced cats

The fashion for miniaturising our pets in one way or another is thought to be associated with a human enthusiasm for animals that have baby-like features. One such facial feature, found in breeds such as the Persian cat, has been increasingly exaggerated in recent years.

Concerns about breeding pets with shortened (brachycephalic) skulls have long been expressed by veterinary surgeons, yet these pets are currently more popular than ever. The internet is full of videos of pugs and French bulldogs trying to nod off while sitting up, sleeping with their tongues hanging out or snoring like a train. These videos aren't funny once you know the root cause of all these behaviours is that the animal is in respiratory distress. Brachycephaly causes a range of unpleasant life-long symptoms from which there is little respite for the sufferer. Essentially, in a flat-faced cat, all the soft tissue (including the soft palate, and the tongue), together with the teeth, is scrunched up into a much smaller space. This has the potential to obstruct the cat's air intake in a number of ways.

We don't yet have as much research about brachycephalic cats as we do on brachycephalic dogs, but we do know that in 20 per cent of brachycephalic cats the nasal turbinates (structures normally found tucked inside your cat's nose) protrude into the throat. That 20 per cent is very close to the 21 per cent ratio of nasopharyngeal turbinates found in brachycephalic dogs. This is an ominous sign that cats are being harmed by shortening their faces in the same way that dogs are.

Brachycephaly is a skull deformity created by humans that offers no benefits to the cats who bear it and considerable disadvantages. Cats are definitely better off with the skull that nature intended. Buying brachycephalic kittens encourages cat breeders to make more of them, so if you have your heart set on a flat-faced breed we hope you will consider adopting your cat from a rescue centre.

Mixed breed vs pure breed

It is becoming increasingly popular in the cat world to create new types of cat by crossing one pure-bred cat breed with another. The offspring of mixed breeding are often referred to as hybrids, although true hybrids are a cross between two different species. We'll have a look at true hybrids in a moment but first let's consider the main differences between pure-bred and mixed-breed cats.

The key benefits of purchasing a pure-bred kitten lie in knowing what your cat will look like when he is grown up, and in some cases what kind of personality he is likely to have. But there are disadvantages too. The different pedigree cat breeds

On average, mixed-breed outlive pure-bred cats.

are all man-made creations and members of each breed are listed on a register. Pure breeding means only mating cats that belong to the same breed register, effectively isolating that breed from all other breeds and creating what biologists refer to as an island population. When there are fewer individuals available to select from, those which are bred from are more likely to have faulty genes in common. And so pedigree cats, like members of any other island population, are more susceptible to a range of genetic health conditions.

One way to reduce these risks is to buy a moggy – a total mix of a cat whose father could have been any tomcat living in the area. The VetCompass project collects data from primary care veterinary practices in the UK and has found that while some pedigree cat breeds are long lived (the Birman for example lives on average 16 years) in general mixed-breed cats outlive pure-bred cats by about one-and-a-half years. A similar study in Australia supports these findings. Longer lifespan tends to be positively associated with better health, which we can see reflected in the difference in insurance premiums.

While seeking out mixed ancestry isn't a guarantee of a healthy cat, it does weight the odds in your favour.

Wildcat hybrids

Exotic wildcats have long been hunted for their beautiful fur, and it is hardly surprising that people have sought ways to create the beautiful spots and stripes of the serval or civet in our domesticated friends. For many owners a part of the appeal of cats is the balance between wildness and domesticity. Wildcat hybrids take this to the extreme, looking to all intents and purposes like a wild creature that just happened to have wandered into a family home. And it's not just their looks that can turn heads, these wildcat hybrids can often have a personality that packs a lot of punch. They aren't for the faint hearted, and can occasionally find themselves the centre of attention for all the wrong reasons.

Hybrid cats sold to members of the public are usually several generations removed from the original cross. Savannahs cats, for example, come from mixing a serval with a domestic cat. When you are looking for a wildcat hybrid, they will be given a designation F1, F2 or F3, etc. This F (which stands for filial) rating explains how many generations removed the offspring is from the wildcat parent – an F5 cat would be far more domestic cat than an F1, for example.

Although the idea of a wildcat hybrid is very appealing, the reality is that the temperament of an F1 mix would not be an appropriate pet for many homes – in fact there are laws restricting the ownership of first generation hybrid cats. You

The Bengal cat is a hybrid breed that owes its exotic stripes and spots to the Asian leopard cat.

may need a licence to keep such a pet in the same way that you would need a licence to keep the wildcat parent.

The best type of cat for your family

There is a lot to consider when you are choosing your new kitten or searching for a rescue cat. Different breeds can have quite distinctive personalities as well as looks, and these are both important factors to most cat owners. But the primary consideration when picking a cat should be health. While some of our pedigree cats have been the victims of harmful breeding practices there are pure breeds that can make wonderful, healthy, happy family pets. In addition to their beauty, many pure-bred cats are extremely affectionate and friendly, even dog-like in their temperament and tolerance of being handled. This can be an added advantage in families with young children.

The key is to avoid breeds with serious physical disabilities such as brachycephaly (flat-face) or chondrodystrophy (dwarfism) embedded into the breed standard, and to seek out breeders that understand the importance of genetic diversity and health testing. We'll go into that more thoroughly in the next chapter.

6

Choosing a Cat

Once you have decided what type of cat you want to bring into your life, you can start on the really exciting part of your journey into cat ownership: finding and choosing your cat.

Most adult cats are adopted from rescue centres, though it is sometimes possible to buy an older cat from a breeder. Kittens are sometimes available in rescue centres but tend to be snapped up quite quickly. Many come from hobby breeders, or from families where a pet cat has had a litter.

In this chapter we look at the pros and cons of adopting a cat or kitten from a rescue centre, and at different ways you can buy from a breeder. We also look at some cat and kitten sources that are best avoided.

The pros and cons of rescue cats

While some authorities have reported that numbers of animals being relinquished to shelters are falling, it's likely that there will be cats needing homes up and down the country for the foreseeable future, and many people feel a sense of responsibility for that problem. Being part of the solution can be very fulfilling and there is no doubt that giving a loving home to any rescue pet is a wonderful thing to do.

There is almost certainly a lovely cat waiting in a rescue centre near you.

However, it must be acknowledged that some rescue cats need special care. They may have behavioural problems that need resolving, or health issues that need addressing. Some won't be suitable for young families, or for homes where the adults are out at work all day. However, there are very many cats available for adoption that have no such issues. And a cat rescue centre near you will almost certainly have a cat that would suit your family.

One of the great benefits of rescuing an adult cat is that you know what you are getting, whereas a kitten may not turn out as you expect. You also won't have to spend a couple months worrying about multiple meals and keeping a tiny one safe and amused.

If you are not sure whether a rescue cat might be right for your family, do give your local cat rescue a ring before you make up your mind. Pippa's previous cat Gadget came from a cat rescue just a few miles from her home and brought over 16 years of joy to her family. You never know, *your* soulmate could be waiting for you just a few miles down the road.

Finding a kitten or cat through rescue

Wanting a kitten doesn't necessarily exclude you from the rescue route but it certainly makes it more challenging. If you don't have your heart set on a particular colour or rare pedigree breed, it's worth scouring your local rescue centres and leaving your details with them. Kittens are regularly relinquished to shelters by unprepared owners who can't find them homes, but they may also be rehomed quickly. Be prepared to contact several centres, to travel some distance if necessary and to wait a while.

Whether you are hoping for a kitten or an adult, the best thing that you can do if you are set on adopting is to start by making a list of what you want in a cat, and what you can offer. Write down the details of your family, home, garden and location. Include other pets, how often you are home and whether the rest of the family is on board with rescuing. The centre will want to see that

Rescue kittens tend to be snapped up quite quickly.

you are all committed to this decision. Be honest when you make this list. Some people try to trick the rescue centre into thinking their home matches a certain cat's criteria, usually genuinely believing that it will be fine once they bring him home. But returns to rescue are sad occasions, and centres endeavour to avoid clashes of this nature. Be aware that most rescue centres will also want to visit your home to make sure that your situation is as you describe.

Choosing your rescue cat

There are a number of charities that provide cat rescue centres in many parts of the world. Pippa found her rescue cat Gadget at a branch of Cats Protection, a leading UK cat charity. Pippa and her family picked Gadget purely on the way she greeted them – she was simply the friendliest cat in the cattery. You may have other criteria, such as markings and colour, but we strongly recommend that you pick a friendly cat, especially if you have young children visiting or living at home.

While there is no 'purchase price' as such for a rescue cat there is a cost. Most rescue centres ask for a significant donation to help them continue their work, and may ask for a larger donation for kittens. If the cat you rescue is very young and has not yet been neutered you will probably be asked to sign an agreement that you will ensure the operation takes place when they are old enough. You may also be asked to agree that you will keep your cat indoors at night.

Pet shop kittens

Beyond the world of rescues, there are a lot of ways to find a kitten. Friends or neighbours, adverts online, pet shops or pure-bred cat breeders. The choices are plentiful, but pet shops are one you should rule out straight away.

Although it's less common these days, some pet shops still do sell kittens. The sight of baby cats miaowing in a small cage, seemingly begging you to bring them home, is bound to tug at your heart strings. We don't think you should succumb to this temptation for several reasons.

When you buy a cat, you want to know that it was raised with loving care, and with health and temperament as the main considerations. All kittens need socialising thoroughly before they are eight weeks old, and that isn't going to happen in a pet shop. A kitten in a pet shop could have come from anywhere. You have no way of knowing what the mother cat's situation is – how often she is allowed to get pregnant and have a litter, what kind of veterinary care she receives and what conditions she is living in. Is she an adored pet who had one litter before being spayed, or a valued member of a specialist cat breeder's family? In both these cases her owner would care desperately about who their babies went home with, but this isn't likely to apply in a pet store kitten.

Sometimes people buy a kitten from a pet shop in order to rescue it, and it can certainly feel like a rescue when you remove that tiny thing from their cramped box and bring them into your loving arms. But sadly it's not that simple, because every time someone buys a kitten from a pet shop that kitten is replaced by another, who is replaced by yet another. And thus the trade grows and grows. Purchasing pet shop kittens is what keeps this trade alive.

Buying a pure-bred kitten or cat from a breeder

While some pure-bred cat breeders will occasionally advertise their kittens on general pet sales websites, most established breeders will not. There are clubs for most pure-bred cat breeds which are often a good initial point of contact for those looking for a kitten. You'll find lists of cat breed clubs provided by organisations such as The International Cat Association, the Governing Council of the Cat Fancy (UK), and the Cat Fanciers' Association (USA). Before you start contacting breeders, make a note of any questions you want to ask them, such as what health tests have their parent cats had. Be prepared to wait for a kitten. Many pedigree breeders will only have one or two litters each year.

For the most part breeders are aware of health issues in their breed and will be making efforts to keep up with the latest developments in health tests, etc. There is one exception, and that is with cats that have conformational defects such as flat faces or dwarfism written into the breed standard. This is a situation where those with responsibility for the health of the kittens they are producing, can sometimes suffer from breed blindness. In other words they may be in denial about the problems the defect may cause.

Buying a home-bred kitten

If you are perfectly happy to buy a kitten of indeterminate ancestry, then finding a local litter of moggies should not be too difficult. Temperament is everything when buying a kitten, and the environment that the cat is raised in plays a powerful part in forming your cat's personality. Seven years ago, when Lucy and her husband decided to bring a cat into their lives, they had just started looking into the options of rescue centres versus breeders when a colleague came to work and told Lucy that their neighbour's cat had unexpectedly given birth. This kind lady had taken in a cat which she had been told had been spayed. A few short weeks later, it became rather obvious that this was not true when several fluffy kittens dropped onto her carpet.

When the kittens were big enough for visitors, at about five weeks old, Lucy and her husband went to meet them and especially their mother. Mum's temperament was amazing, she came straight up to greet them purring loudly, and was quite happy for her kittens to be fussed. She was a tabby, and the kittens were a really mixed bag. Some short haired, some long haired, and several different colours. The owner clearly loved the surprise family, and had a couple of other pets who were also loved and well cared for.

The kittens spent those early weeks growing up in the heart of a family, with dogs and children surrounding them each day. They were active, bright eyed and, like all kittens, totally gorgeous. Lucy and her husband brought home the little black and white furball three weeks later, and Oscar turned out to have the same fantastic friendly temperament that his mother had. The relationship between the neighbour and Lucy's colleague created a relatively high degree of trust, and Oscar had been vet checked, flea treated and wormed. This kind of situation is as good as any you are likely to find, and gives you an idea of the kind of home environment you are looking for.

Avoiding fake adverts

If you don't know anyone whose cat is expecting kittens, another option is to browse the adverts online. There is nothing intrinsically wrong with buying a kitten from an advertisement, either online or in your local paper. This is how Pippa found Billy. But there are definitely pitfalls that you need to avoid as not all adverts are genuine.

Dishonest people sometimes find a few cute pictures of kittens, pop them up into an advert with 'ready to go now' in the description and usually not a lot else.

When you email or phone they will give various reasons as to why they need a deposit, or even the full amount, upfront before you visit. They will say that people have let them down before, or imply that they are inundated with requests and the kittens will all be gone if you don't do what they ask. They might be quite convincing, when in reality the kittens don't exist at all. You will then be fobbed off with excuses for a few days or weeks until they stop responding at all. This is a common enough scam for the big online selling sites to have prominent warnings, giving examples of the cons they have seen before. Don't get caught out!

One quick way to check whether an image has been stolen or used before, and does not depict real kittens for sale, is to run a Google image search. Go to Google Images and click on the camera symbol in the search box, it will now invite you to paste the image URL or upload a photograph. Do this, and you will then be given a list of results. Some kittens may be listed on more than one site at the same time and this isn't a cause for concern. But if the photos have been used before, in a date before the kittens would even have been born, you know it's time to move on with your search. Avoid anyone who asks for a deposit before you have met the kittens and their mother.

Anyone who cares for their cat will want to meet you before allowing you to buy one of their precious babies. A lack of emotional connection to their kittens, and an absence of interest in you and your situation, is a bad sign too. As is the offer to meet you halfway and sell you a kitten out of the back of a car.

If the owner is keen to meet you and obviously interested in the welfare of her kittens, the next step is to visit the mother cat and her babies in their home. This will give you a chance to make sure you are happy with the conditions in which the kittens are being raised.

The importance of socialisation

One of the chief aims of the first visit to a litter, whether in a family home or at a breeder's cattery, is to make sure that the kittens are being socialised. Cats and dogs need to undergo this process called socialisation when they are very young – it can only take place during a short window of time when baby animals are very willing to accept new experiences and make new friends. When the critical period for socialisation ends, kittens and puppies become fearful of new experiences and therefore slow to make friends. It's important to note that this window of time is much shorter in cats, and is virtually closed by the time kittens leave for their new homes. That means you are entirely dependent on the breeder to make sure that your pet will grow up confident and friendly.

The importance of buying a properly socialised kitten cannot be overstressed. If you bring a nervous puppy home at eight weeks old, you still have some chance of turning him or her into a friendly confident adult. Your chances of doing the same with an untamed terrified eight-week-old kitten are much smaller, simply because the critical period for socialisation in cats is much shorter. Genes matter too, of course. If both of your kitten's parents are friendly, the chances of the kitten growing up friendly increases. But if the kitten has not been well socialised by eight weeks of age, you are going to have problems. The *only* way to be sure your kitten has been raised among family and friends from a young age, and fully socialised before leaving their mother, is to visit them in person when they are still small.

Visiting a litter of kittens

When visiting the litter, make a note of where the kittens spend time. Young kittens need to be raised with people and normal household noises. A litter of kittens raised in a dark barn or shed with little human contact is not going to produce the ideal family pet. Unless you have a lot of time and patience and are experienced in animal behaviour modification techniques, avoid rescued feral kittens. These cats are very challenging to tame and are unlikely to become friendly pets. Look for signs that the kittens you are visiting do actually live indoors and haven't just been brought in for your benefit. Are their toys, litter boxes and food bowls around? Have ornaments been removed and the cat flap locked? A pristine home with no sign of kitten activity should be regarded with suspicion.

If you are buying a pedigree kitten remember to ask to see health certificates when you visit. Look for evidence that the necessary DNA tests for this breed

have been carried out and that the results are satisfactory. Focus on the mother cat, and father cat too if he is there. Look for a friendly confident greeting, with no trace of nervousness. A head bump or some purring in your direction is an added bonus. If you decide to book a kitten then you'll probably need to pay a deposit at this point. You'll also need to choose which kitten you want!

Make sure farm-bred or outdoor kittens have been properly socialised.

Picking out a kitten

If you are happy with your new cat's family and home circumstances when you visit, then it's decision time. Which one to pick? It's so hard to choose! There may be both females and males available. Knowing in advance whether you want a girl or a boy will help narrow the field down. Female cats are nearly twice as expensive to neuter as male cats, and some studies have shown that male cats may be more likely to have a friendly temperament. On the other hand, we have known many affectionate girl cats, and breeding together with good socialisation at a young age are the main influencing factors on your cat's personality. If you like an easy life, and aren't fussy about colour or hair length, go for a short-haired boy.

Kittens should be clean and sweet smelling with bright clear eyes. Whatever sex your kitten is, make sure that they are confident and friendly. There should be no trace of nervousness or jumpiness at your arrival, and the kittens should be purring, active and happy to be handled.

Arranging to collect your cat

Two months is considered the minimum age at which a kitten should be separated from its mother. The Department for the Environment and Rural Affairs in the UK published a code of practice for the welfare of cats in 2017 which states that a kitten 'cannot be sold under eight weeks'. And the sale of kittens under 8 weeks old is illegal in some states in the USA. Many pedigree cat breeders won't let their kittens go until they are twelve weeks old. While most mixed-breed cat owners rehome their kittens at eight weeks, some may try and offload them at an earlier age. It's a good idea to familiarise yourself with what an eight-week-old kitten looks like in case someone tries to pull the wool over your eyes. In general, expect to collect your kitten at about eight weeks.

Final preparations

If you are not fussy about what type of cat you want, your local rescue centre is a great place to start. And if you have your heart set on the pitter patter of very tiny paws, your first priorities need to be socialisation and health. Be firm with yourself and don't be tempted to take on the project of 'taming' a feral kitten unless you are very experienced in this area.

7

Final Preparations

One of the joys of cat ownership is that you don't need to spend too much money on products. You can keep a cat happy and healthy with very little equipment. There are things to do and buy before bringing your cat or kitten home, but don't worry, you won't need to redesign your home, or spend a fortune. Although there are a great many products aimed at cat owners, most aren't necessary. Indeed, some of the more expensive purchases you may be tempted to make are likely to end up gathering dust at the back of a cupboard, while other simpler items can make your life much easier. In this chapter we'll identify the equipment you need and look at some of the general preparations you need to make to create a 'cat-friendly' environment.

The 'airlock'

It's a particularly good idea to think about safety precautions before your cat arrives, not least because it's quite difficult to think clearly with a new kitten zooming around your home or while trying to tempt a terrified rescue cat out from behind the sofa. Both adult cats and kittens are masters at slipping through the tiniest of spaces. Even if your cat is going to be allowed outdoors later on, you'll need to keep him shut in for the first few weeks to prevent kittens being harmed, and to prevent older cats attempting to find their way back to their previous homes. If you can, restrict your family to going in and out of your home through a double set of doors, such as an enclosed hall or porch, as this helps prevent your new arrival escaping. Treat the area as an 'airlock' (children can play space ships) and make sure everyone closes one door before they open the other.

The safe room

It's a great idea to set aside a room in your home where your new cat or kitten will spend his first few days. The idea of a safe room is that it creates a space for your new cat that fulfils a number of important functions. A safe room is a place:

- That other pets can't access
- With no direct access to outdoors
- Where the cat is always within a few feet of a litter box
- Without inaccessible spaces where your cat can get trapped.

Your cat's safe room should ideally have a baby gate across the door to deny access to small children and dogs. While your kitten and your dog may well become great friends in the future, the manner of those first few meetings are very important. With a suitably managed safe space, when you begin to leave the door open your cat can venture out on his terms and return whenever he feels worried. If you are getting a kitten, he'll be able to simply walk between the bars of the gate when the door is open. If you are bringing home a larger cat, you might want to choose a baby gate with a small cat door in the bottom. These are readily available, but remember that this solution won't work if your dog is small too!

Most cats and virtually all kittens are quite capable of climbing up inside a chimney, and getting a scared kitten down from one is something of a challenge. So if you have an open fireplace in your safe room, as Pippa did in her office when she brought Billy home, you are going to need to block the chimney up. If the fireplace has a flat surround, you may be able to put a board across it, but many fireplaces are quite decorative. If that is the case you'll need to stuff something up inside the entrance to the flue. Make sure it can easily be removed later – and don't forget to take it down before you next light the fire!

All new cats need to spend a few weeks confined to the house. Even if your cat will be given access to outdoors once he has settled in, he'll need toilet facilities indoors for this period of time. This means a litter box and a good supply of cat litter is essential.

Choosing a cat litter box

Litter boxes have gone high tech. In addition to the traditional plain plastic box, there are now boxes with lids, boxes with doors, automatic boxes, boxes that look like miniature cement mixers and litter systems that look like tiny toilets and need to be 'plumbed in'. You can even buy purpose-built cupboards with a cat shaped entrance to conceal the litter box entirely.

A box with extra high sides can stop the litter from spreading out when your cat digs, but it can also be off-putting to a new cat. There is no point in having a high-sided box that litter can't escape from if your cat doesn't want to get in it. Your priority should be to make it as simple to use as possible – as clear to the cat as it can be that this is the place for him to pee. Pippa wanted a box with a lid and a door for Billy in order reduce odour and keep her spaniels out of the cat litter. She left the lid and door off the box to begin with to make sure that Billy was not deterred from using his new bathroom facilities. Once your cat is using the box happily on a regular basis, the lid can be added. Then, a few days later, the door. These simple precautions help to prevent litter box training problems.

Choosing cat litter

When it comes to picking cat litter there are a lot of different options. From dust-free to clumping, odour-reducing to lightweight, the options on the shelves can be baffling. And different cats may well prefer different types. You can even find cat litter that claims to be safe to flush down the loo, although there are very mixed opinions on whether this is a good idea for your plumbing or the environment. Pippa used pine-based litter for Billy to mask odours, which he was fine with, but some cats might not like the smell. When Oscar was small Lucy found the non-clumping litter to be easiest to manage. But if you are going to be in close contact with the litter box then a pine option might be best.

There are also a range of litter scoops available. We recommend choosing one that is sturdy and not likely to break after a few uses, that is fairly deep so the litter doesn't risk falling out and has a long handle to save your back and knees from repeatedly bending over. You can choose between metal or plastic, with a variety of types of holes in them to help you pick up the poop but leave the untouched litter behind.

Food and water

We will look at feeding your cat in much more detail in Chapter 10: Feeding Your Cat, so this is just a brief summary of what you need to buy in advance. Cats are obligate carnivores, which means that they should just be eating meat products, or food specifically designed for cats. You'll need some wet cat food (sold in pouches) labelled as suitable for your cat's age (most brands do kitten, adult and senior versions). If possible, start off with the same brand that the previous owner used. This will help to ease your new cat's transition from his old home to yours. Moving is stressful for cats, just as it is for people, and upset stomachs are common in the early days, so the fewer things in your cat's life that are new or different, the better. To switch brands, wait a few weeks and then combine the old and new food for a couple of days before changing over completely.

Choosing a cat bowl can be fun, and there are some great designs about. While cats will happily eat off our plates, most of us choose to provide them with something we won't be using ourselves. Some kittens get food caught under their chins and find it difficult to keep themselves clean if fed from a small deep sided bowl to begin with. This happened to Billy, who developed a kind of sticky beard at one point, so Pippa always fed him from a plate. Like many cats, Billy is quite a careful eater and has never spilled food. Some cats like to lift chunks of food out of their bowls and place it daintily on the floor for further inspection. If your cat turns out to be a 'food spreader' like Oscar you can buy a wipeable plastic mat, in cute cat designs, to go under their food bowls.

Buying food bowls in pairs is a good idea. One can be in the dishwasher while the other is in use. Ceramic bowls are great for staying in one place. They are heavy and don't tip up easily, they are easy to clean and widely available, but they are breakable. If you live with kids and want them to be involved with feeding your cat, you'll need something that won't shatter if it gets dropped. Stainless steel bowls are similarly easy to clean, but they can slide around while your cat is eating depending upon what type of flooring you use. Rubber rims remove this problem, and any stainless steel design is fairly indestructible. The cheapest option, however, is usually a plastic bowl. And while they may not last as long as china or stainless steel, they are great for families like Oscar's where children like to help feed the cat.

It's important that you make sure your cat always has clean fresh drinking water available. Many cats fed on wet food drink very little and cat owners often worry about their pet not drinking. We'll talk a bit more about how much a cat should drink in the health chapter, but it's worth mentioning at this point that some cats prefer to drink running water, and as a result some cat owners find kitty water fountains helpful. They come in some pretty funky designs and are easy to get hold of online.

Scratching posts

If you don't provide your cat with a purpose-built scratching area, they will scratch your furniture and carpets. This isn't a maybe: it will happen. Cats have an instinctive need to pull and scrape their claws across a rough surface. They especially love to do this on any kind of basketwork: so if you have an antique wicker basket that you don't want damaged, put it away for the time being. Fortunately, cats also like to give their claws a good workout on anything made from coarse string or rope. You'll need to provide enough of these scratching posts so that your new cat doesn't have to go far to find one. If you get this right, most cats will use what you provide rather than your best furniture.

Pippa started Billy off with a small tent-shaped scratcher, which he also liked to use for an evening nap. He also has a well-worn scratcher that is suspended from a cupboard door handle in the hall. Once they are allowed outdoors most cats will find themselves a few choice scratching posts – Oscar's favourite is an old tree stump in the garden where he spends a few moments each day.

Cats like to get their claws into a wicker basket.

This wooden puzzle box provided Billy with hours of fun.

Cat toys

Buying and making cat toys is a lot of fun, especially with kittens – cats become less playful as they mature. At six months old, Billy would still play for long periods of time with his favourite toys, but by the time he was a year old he had lost interest in most of them. For many cats, loss of interest in toys coincides with the point at which they start to hunt outdoors, and you may find that an indoor cat will continue to play with toys for longer than one that has access to your garden.

One of the toys that Billy enjoyed most as a kitten was a wooden box with holes in the sides and top. We filled the box with small toys and balls, and Billy spent a happy half hour hooking them all out with his paws.

Tiny toys filled with catnip are very appealing to many cats – though it's worth remember that the 'buzz' that some cats get from catnip is an inherited trait and not all cats have it. Billy and Oscar are both attracted to catnip and that means catnip toys are a favourite with them.

Most kittens will spend a lot of time playing with tiny balls and springs. In fact anything that moves easily when patted with a paw. Of the more expensive toys, Billy's favourite was an enclosed track that houses a flashing ball. There are holes in the track so that the cat can put his paw in and get the ball moving again, but he can't remove the ball entirely.

One of the toys that cats find most appealing is the most simple, and that is a cardboard box with a hole cut in the side and a few novel items in it – such as Billy's wooden box above. Scrunched-up packing paper is fine. Billy at two years old still enjoys playing in and exploring any packaging from things that have been delivered to the house.

Cat beds

The range of cat beds available online is enough to make your head spin. From a simple blanket on the floor to multi-tiered cave-like structures. You don't need to buy a cat bed if you don't want to, but if you do, make sure that you buy one which is machine washable. Oscar spent every night sucking his bed when he arrived home, and it frequently needed refreshing over those early months. Some cats enjoy den-style beds. Billy loved his kitten caves when he was small. These days, like Oscar, he prefers to stretch out on a human bed or snooze on the sofa. Many cats are huge fans of faux-sheepskin surfaces, and a bed or chair lined with this kind of fabric is often popular.

Cat furniture

There has been an explosion in the availability of designer cat furniture in the last few years. From simple perches to elaborate state-of-the-art built-in cat stairways and balconies, where your furry friend can wander aloft to his heart's content. A visit to Pinterest will reveal the true extent of these masterpieces and the only limitation is your wallet and your imagination.

It's true that cats love to be up high, and they are excellent climbers. It's also true that your cat won't suffer if his main available perch is the top of the fridge, and he'll soon figure out how to travel around most of your rooms via the tops of the furniture without ever touching the ground. If DIY is your thing, you may decide to build some cat furniture yourself, but it's certainly worth looking at what is available commercially for inspiration and ideas.

Most cats appreciate a perch from which to look down on the world.

Either way, you don't need to worry about installing cat furniture for a new kitten. In fact it's probably best if your kitten's options for getting himself out of your reach are fairly limited to begin with.

The cat carrier

There are a few different types of cat carrier on the market right now, and if you are picking up a tiny new kitten it probably doesn't matter too much which one you choose. It isn't very difficult to get a kitten into a carrier. If your new friend is well socialised and confident they will slip right in through a front-opening door without too many objections. Older cats can be more of a challenge and need a strong cat-proof container.

If you are bringing home an adult rescue cat you might need to consider forgoing a front-opening carrier in favour of one that opens at the top. With most modern plastic carriers, the entire top half can be detached from the bottom, and you can lower your cat in via a much bigger opening. This prevents that classic limbs-splayed pose that prevents you from sliding the cat into a smaller door. Some of the traditional wicker-picnic-basket style carriers flap open at the top too, but it is easier for a cat to grip onto the sides of wicker and create resistance. Some cats will attempt to escape from a carrier, so avoid the temporary cardboard carriers for older, poorly socialised cats. Especially if you have a long journey and don't fancy your furry friend joining you on the dashboard.

Keep it simple

A new cat joining your family needn't involve you in extensive alterations to your home. Creating a temporary safe space is the key to success. We recommend you start simple, choose your safe room and install a baby gate if you have small kids or other pets. Buy a big basic litter box with high sides at the back and some low-odour cat litter, and buy the same cat or kitten food they are already on. Add a few small balls, catnip mice and springs, a scratching post and a soft warm blanket, and you are ready to go. You can add all the fancy paraphernalia you want later on.

Now on to Part 2, where we'll begin by settling in your new friend and introducing him to the family.

2

Life With
Your Cat

8

Settling In

Bringing your new cat home is an exciting and often long-awaited moment. The aim of this chapter is to make sure everything goes smoothly for you during those initial few weeks and to get you off to a flying start with your new pet. We'll be looking at common problems that most new cat owners face, such as introducing a kitten to other pets and small children, and helping an anxious cat feel at home.

You probably realise that it isn't a good idea to allow a new kitten or cat to go exploring outdoors on his first day! A kitten outside alone might get lost, stolen or hurt, and the chances of an older, newly rescued, cat packing his bags and heading for his previous home are high. So for the next few days at least you'll be getting to know your new cat in his safe space and gradually introducing him to the rest of your home, as you help him to adapt to his new life as part of your family.

Collecting your cat

It isn't safe to travel with a cat loose in a car no matter how calm or friendly he may be, so you will need to use a pet carrier or travel crate. Line the carrier with an old towel or blanket to stop your cat sliding around, but don't use anything special, as a stressed cat can sometimes have accidents on the journey home. Your cat has yet to discover that he is on his way to the best home on the planet and is likely to be upset, so expect a certain amount of noise from your new housemate on the journey.

Arriving in a new home

Creating a calm and welcoming environment for your cat or kitten is important, and there a number of practical steps you can take to minimise stress for him during his first few weeks with you. When you arrive home, grab a bag of tasty cat treats and take the cat carrier into the safe room you have prepared. Check that the windows are shut and close the door to the room so that the cat can't make a break for it. Now it's time to open the carrier and see if he is ready to make friends! What happens next will depend very much on the individual cat.

Open the door, or lift the lid off the carrier, and wait for the cat to come out at his own pace. Some cats will come straight out, others may be very frightened. A scared cat will often try to make himself appear small. His eyes will look big – pupils dilated – and his ears will be flat. He may press his body against the side or floor of the carrier. He may hiss or spit, and even try to bite or scratch if handled. Don't attempt to remove a cat in this state! Just leave him in peace with a bowl of water and a dish of food. There is no hurry and we promise your cat will not still be hiding in that travel basket in three weeks' time.

Many cats emerge slowly and cautiously over the space of a few minutes. After ten minutes or so, if your new friend is still hiding in the carrier, you can try to tempt him out with a little food. Try offering a treat or a fingertip dipped in wet cat food. Don't worry if it is refused at this point.

Let your cat set the pace – it takes time to make friends.

Kittens are usually less of a challenge. Pippa tempted Billy out of his travel crate with a little wet kitten food on the end of her fingers. He licked this off inside the carrier to begin with then gradually followed her fingers out into the room and began to explore. It may help if you sit on the floor to make yourself look less threatening before trying to encourage your cat to come and say hello. If your cat is confident enough to explore the safe room straight away, try not to interrupt him. He needs to map out his new territory, check out the availability of litter box and food, and make sure there is nothing dangerous lurking there.

A place to hide

Once your cat has plucked up the courage to come out and survey his surroundings you may be tempted to remove the carrier from the room. But he still needs a refuge to return to whenever he feels insecure. A nervous cat may need to hide again every time someone comes into the room for the first day or two, or whenever anyone makes a sudden movement. Removing the hiding place will make him more nervous rather than less, as being able to hide makes the cat feel safe, giving him a secure base from which to explore. A simple cardboard box with a soft blanket inside can also work as a hidey hole – you can even tape the lid closed and make a hole in the side as a doorway.

Anxious cats need a place to hide.

It is great when a cat makes friends quickly, but the depth of your future friendship does not seem to be associated with the speed of this early settling in process. When Pippa brought her rescue cat Gadget home, the designated safe room was the utility room. Gadget spent the best part of three days hiding behind the washing machine, eating and using the litter box in secret. Yet within a couple of weeks she had transformed herself into the most affectionate, confident and sociable family pet – take heart and be patient.

Mealtimes

Many a friendship has been formed over meals, and cats are no different from most of us. Cats can be picky at times about the kind of food they prefer, but most have a hearty appetite and cannot resist for long a human who regularly feeds them. Feeding your new cat as often as possible during the first few days helps build his confidence and trust in you.

This happens naturally with kittens as they need several meals a day, and each of those meals is an opportunity to build your new friendship. Adult cats can cope with larger meals and you can safely feed your older cat once in the morning and once in the evening. However, if you are at home there is no reason why you shouldn't divide an adult cat's daily food ration into many small portions too. There is no such thing as 'too many meals'. This will give you more opportunities to bond. Just make sure that the total amount of food being consumed over a 24-hour period is the right amount for your cat's needs. You'll find detailed information on what to feed, how much and when, in Chapter 10: Feeding Your Cat.

The first night

Some cats will want to spend their first night in the cat carrier or hiding place you have provided for them. If your cat is already confidently exploring the safe room on the first day then the chances are they will want to sleep somewhere higher up, such as a cupboard top, bed or windowsill. Beware of putting carriers or a cat bed up on high surfaces unless they are securely attached or on a broad non-slip surface – many cats like to knead the fabric of their bed with their paws as they go off to sleep and this can cause beds and boxes to move around. You can leave a cushion or cat bed on a low chair if you want to, but there's no guarantee your cat will use it.

With very small kittens you may feel happier to know that they are secure at night. Some kittens will be happy to sleep shut in their carrier from when you go to bed until you get up. Provided you don't leave the kitten too long (more than six hours or so) this can work well. Billy slept in his cat carrier for several weeks after Pippa brought him home at eight weeks old. Older cats are unlikely to be happy with this arrangement, so just leave the carrier door open for them to choose where they want to sleep.

Getting checked over

Within a day or two of arriving home it is time to take your cat to the vet for his first check-up. This is really important both in terms of vaccinations and to make sure your new pet is in good health. Fleas, mites and even bigger issues, such as potential heart conditions, need to be flagged up straight away so that they can be managed.

Billy waiting patiently for his first vet check.

Although some vets have open hours where you can drop by, it's best to book a visit with your new pet before you bring him home. This ensures that this important check-up doesn't get forgotten or put off in all of that new-pet excitement. Your cat won't thank you for introducing him to his medical arrangements, but it has to be done. The experience will soon be forgotten once your friendship begins to blossom.

Building trust

It's fine to leave your cat alone in the safe room. You don't have to sit in there with him until he is ready to come out of the carrier if you don't want to. Once your cat trusts you enough not to hide when you enter the room and is happy to eat in front of you, you are well on your way. Signs that your cat regards you as a friend include the cat approaching you and rubbing his body against yours and purring when stroked. But even at this point, it still pays to take things slowly. Studies have shown that interactions between people and cats actually last longer if initiated by the cat. In other words, playing hard to get at this point may work in your favour – a certain amount of pretend indifference on your part may hasten the bonding process.

Beyond the safe room

Once your cat is settled and confident in the safe room he is ready to expand his horizons. If you have no other pets or small children then as soon as your cat is using his litter box regularly, eating in front of you, purring and happy to be handled by family members, then it's time to allow him to explore.

Again, you need to take some precautions, because cats are masters of escape. He may look the picture of innocence tucking into his jellied meat chunks, but Houdini had nothing on your cat. That tiny high up window in the spare bedroom, the one you thought didn't matter, or wasn't open wide enough to count? That's the one your cat will go through. So before you let your new cat out of his safe room it is vital that your entire family have been drilled in the art of squeezing through doors without letting the cat follow them, and wherever possible you should make sure that there are always two closed doors – the airlock – between the cat and the outside world.

Remember, your cat can jump higher than you think, slip past people's legs in a blink of an eye and can get through a space you'd struggle to push your arm through. So close all the windows and exterior doors in your home. Issue threats of dire punishment for any family member leaving windows open, and if you have a kitten stick a note on the bathroom door telling everyone to put the toilet seat down before leaving the bathroom. Fishing a half-drowned soggy kitten out of a toilet bowl is almost as upsetting for you as it is for the cat.

How long does it take for a cat to settle in?

Billy was running around his safe room, exploring and playing, within his first hour. But he was just eight weeks old and had been well socialised in a noisy, busy family. Some shelter cats will need two or three days before they venture out from their hiding place; a very scared cat may need more time.

Oscar was also from a bustling family, but he took a little longer than Billy to settle in. Although he explored straight away it was very tentative, and he needed lots of reassurance. It was a good couple of days before he seemed to be really confident and self-assured. Pippa's rescue cat Gadget was around two or three years old when she came home. Like many shelter cats she needed several days before venturing out from her hiding place.

Every cat is different, of course, and your experience won't necessarily mirror ours. Remember initial hesitance is not necessarily a reflection on a cat's personality.

Friends at last

These first few days require a little patience. Don't worry if your cat doesn't leap into your lap on the day you meet, as most take a while to accept new people as their friends. Remember that you have been planning and thinking about this for a while but your cat needs time to adjust. Friendship will come and when it does it will be worth the wait.

Being part of a family doesn't just mean forming friendships with a number of different humans, in many cases it means learning to get along with other pets too. The presence of other animals in the home can complicate things a little because your cat will need a chance to adjust to them. Let's take a look at, where appropriate, how best to make those introductions.

9
Meeting the Family

I n the security of the safe room your cat has been able to get to know the human members of his new family. Once he leaves the protection of the safe room there will be a whole new world for him to explore, and in many families there will be new four-legged friends to meet too. If you already have a cat, dog or other pets at home, this chapter is for you.

Protecting small pets

There are certain animals that will need to be kept apart from your new friend on a permanent basis. These include small rodents and insects. How vulnerable they are to your cat will depend in part on their size and in part on their temperament.

Oscar shares his home and garden with a host of guinea pigs, who usually ignore him and he ignores them. Initially he did try to poke a paw or two through the bars, but now pays them very little attention. However, Oscar also shares his home with a hamster, who needs protecting from him.

Hamsters are particularly appealing to cats, and most will happily spend hours on end staring at them. Simply living in a house with a cat has been shown in some studies to be stressful to small rodents such as hamsters, mice and rats. It's important to remember that your cat is a predator at heart and that these small pets are his natural prey. Don't try to introduce your cat to these tiny animals, or be tempted to convince yourself that the cat wouldn't hurt them because they are used to each other. This will only end in heartbreak. Make sure that children's rooms with small pets in them are out of bounds to your cat. And that cages are heavy and secure so that if someone inadvertently lets the cat into the room, they cannot push the cage over or pull the lid off. A split second is all it takes for your predatory friend to turn your beloved hamster into a mid-afternoon snack.

Fish bowls are another source of fascination too. Any aquarium you have in your home will need to be heavy enough for the cat to be incapable of moving it, and fitted with a secure, cat-proof lid.

Remember also that while larger pets such as guinea pigs may not be afraid of your cat it is important to always ensure that their run is secure. Once a cat knows that they are unattainable they will usually leave larger pets, such as rabbits and guinea pigs, alone. But don't be tempted to relax your guard and tell yourself that they are friends. If the lid were removed it could be a very different story. Cats can and do kill rabbits and it's best to assume that any pet smaller than your cat is at risk. Fortunately, with a few sensible security precautions you should be able to keep your larger outdoor pets happy, even with a cat around.

Dogs and cats

Dogs are of course a very different matter. Your dog and cat will almost certainly be sharing the same space, and will want a similar sort of attention from the rest of the family, so it's important that we help them to get off on the right foot. Remember, dogs vary greatly in their reaction to cats. However, with time, patience and good management, most will be able to live comfortably side by side with their new feline housemate, even if they never end up being close friends. Let's take a look at how to make that transition.

Firstly, you need to allow the cat to decide on how the introductions will progress. Make sure that it is impossible for the dog to physically get to the cat, and give the cat the ability to escape from the dog if he feels the need. A good way to do this with all but the tiniest of dogs or the largest of cats is to use a baby gate, with the dog on one side and the cat on the other. Kittens

Oscar ignores the guinea pigs but they foolishly want to be friends.

and small cats will be able to slip through the bars of the gate and the dog will be unable to follow. Many larger cats will jump the gate, but if your cat is not willing to do that you may need to choose a gate with a small cat door in the bottom.

Put the gate across the entrance to the cat's safe room and leave the door to the room open. Begin by just allowing the dog to see the cat through the barrier, and observe how they react. Make sure that the cat can retreat into his safe space and that the dog is unable to follow. Don't underestimate the ability of quite small dogs to jump over baby gates and make sure you supervise first interactions. If either shows signs of aggression, or the dog is very overexcited by the presence of the cat, then keep the barrier in place for now.

The amount of time for which you will need to separate the two will vary depending upon how they both react. The first time Billy saw Pippa's Labrador Tess, through the baby gate and across his room, he arched his back, and with all his hair on end hissed bravely and loudly at her. This is a pretty normal reaction for a kitten that has never seen a dog before. Yet they were best friends within a week. So don't worry too much about how your cat reacts to the dog. More important is the dog's reaction to the cat.

It can be tempting to misinterpret your dog's reaction to the cat. We all want to think that our beloved pooch would never harm a hair on a kitten's head, but that is not always the case. The nicest of dogs can behave inappropriately

Puppies and kittens raised together can become great
friends. Older dogs may take a little more time.

towards a cat. The best outcome is a dog that is mildly interested and amused by your kitten, you'll see a relaxed body posture in this dog accompanied by a gently wagging tail. There are three key types of inappropriate reaction. One is overly boisterous rough play, another is fear and the third is aggression.

Pippa's Labrador Rachael fell into the first of these categories. When Billy was very tiny she treated him like a cuddly toy, getting excited around him, poking him quite hard with her nose, attempting to chase him when he moved. Though her tail was wagging and she wasn't afraid of him, there was a very real risk of her chasing and grabbing him. Possibly with devastating consequences. For the next couple of weeks she was only allowed to greet Billy on a lead. And for another few weeks after that, under close supervision. They are now great friends, but the process of arriving at that point required a lot more input from Pippa's family in order to ensure Billy's safety.

A dog that is frightened of cats may snap at a kitten if the kitten won't leave them alone. This dog needs to be given plenty of opportunity to withdraw from the kitten until their concerns have subsided.

The dog that poses the greatest threat to a kitten is a dog with a high level of prey drive and a strong compulsion to chase moving objects. A dog that sees a cat as a prey object is unlikely to be able to relax around them. The dog may freeze into a rigid body posture with their eyes 'locked' onto the cat. There will probably be no wagging tail. There is no doubt that a dog like this could attack a kitten aggressively with little warning, and is also a threat to an adult cat. If you suspect you have this problem it is important to get professional advice on whether or not your pets can be safely integrated and on how to introduce them.

When you are confident that your dog is not a threat to your cat, and when your cat is relaxed around the dog, you take down the baby gate that separates them. However, there are benefits to leaving the gate in place, as many dogs like to snack on the contents of a cat's litter box.

Introducing cats to other cats

Introducing cats to one another requires patience and a willingness to accept that success is not guaranteed. Resident cats are almost always quite stressed by the appearance of a new cat in their home, though many do adapt in time. Don't attempt introductions until the new cat is settled and happy in their room. Before you bring the two cats face to face, most experts recommend that you carry out a 'scent swapping' procedure for several days in a row.

Introducing a new cat to your resident cat needs to be done carefully.

Scent is an important means of communication for cats and they scent mark by rubbing themselves on objects or animals that they wish to be associated with. Scent swapping means taking the scent of your new cat and rubbing it on areas of your home used by your resident cat, and vice versa. You can use a cushion or blanket to do this, or if they are happy with this you can stroke one cat repeatedly on their face and then rub your scented hand on furniture in the other cat's area of the home. You can also try offering each cat some treats from your hand that is scented with the other cat.

After a few days, once the cats show no aversive reaction to each other's scent, you can move on to the next step. Pop your new cat into a pet carrier and put him in a room not accessible to the resident cat, and then let the resident cat explore the safe room where his prospective house-mate has been living. Do this at a time when he is hungry, and offer him small treats at intervals in this room.

At another time, when your resident cat is out or crated, and your new cat is hungry, allow the new cat to explore the rest of the house. Again, offer small treats at intervals. What you are trying to do is reduce anxiety over the alien new scent and to associate it with something pleasurable.

If you have taught your resident cat to go into a crate willingly for treats (see Chapter 13, Training and Tricks), then the next step is to crate your resident cat and place him in the safe room with the new cat. Try to keep both cats distracted with food, and introductions brief. If there is no hissing and spitting you are well on your way, and ready to move to the final step of introducing the cats in person.

Supervise these introductions and give both cats the opportunity to back away to their own part of the house. You can't expect the cats to be friends from the start – it is most unlikely that they will want to spend time together initially – and your aim should be to distract them and get them to ignore one another. Your role is to ensure they don't hurt one another, and that integrating the two cats doesn't cause behaviour problems in either of them.

Once you allow your new cat to leave his room you need to lock any cat doors to prevent him going outside. You will have to think of ways of ensuring that someone is on hand to let your established cat in and out, without permitting the new cat to escape.

Getting along

Introducing adult cats to one another can be very challenging, and it is not unusual to need professional advice from your vet or a cat behaviourist. Even if introductions go relatively smoothly it's important to give each cat their own personal space, and their own litter box. In some cases, cats that have been introduced as adults will become friends, in other's you'll need to settle for them simply getting along. With dogs, the outcome may be more promising. Many family dogs are receptive to being friends with a cat, and most cats don't seem to view dogs as competition. Billy quite likes the dogs he lives with and seeks out their company, and dogs and kittens that grow up together can become very good friends indeed.

10

Feeding Your Cat

All of the 40 or so wildcat species living natural lives around the world have something in common with your cat, and that's their adaptation to a specialised diet. Cats are what is known as obligate carnivores. This means that they really do need to eat meat, and can thrive solely on meat together with other bits and pieces of animals, such as ligaments and bone. Raw feeding enthusiasts like to replicate this diet by providing their cat with a balanced mixture of raw meat, bones and other organs, sometimes referred to as the whole prey model of feeding. It can work very well for cats in some circumstances, and we'll help you figure out whether or not this is something you might like to try. For most of us, a commercial brand of cat food will be the mainstay of our cat's diet.

In this chapter we'll take a look at the natural feeding habits and patterns of cats and at how we can work with those feline instincts to keep our friends healthy and well fed. We'll talk about how to choose the right type of food for your cat, how much to feed, and give you some examples of mealtime schedules for kittens.

Are cats picky eaters?

Cats have a reputation for being picky eaters. If you give a cat the same thing to eat repeatedly, they may begin to refuse it. This is a natural behaviour displayed by many domestic cats. Scientists call it the monotony effect. Preferring variety makes sense for wildcats and helps to ensure a broad range of nutrients in their diet. It may also help to avoid a build-up of toxins if the wrong food is consumed. In the wild this instinct helps to keep cats safe and healthy.

Of course, the domestic cat doesn't need to worry about getting the right nutrients if you provide him with a well-designed complete food. But your cat doesn't know that. The monotony effect can be frustrating for owners, who think they've got a set routine for feeding and find their cat suddenly turning up his nose at the brand of kitty food that was previously flavour of the month. One way to avoid this problem is to get your cat accustomed to three or four different brands of food and rotate them.

Choosing the right type of cat food

There are four main options when it comes to feeding your cat. The first three are available from pet stores and supermarkets. The fourth requires more effort on your part:

- Wet food sold in pouches or trays
- Dry food sold in boxes or bags
- A combination of wet and dry
- Raw food.

Deciding which type of food to give your cat is not straightforward. There are pros and cons to each type of feeding, for you as well as for your cat.

Dry food vs wet food

Dry cat food, often known as kibble, is a very common choice and with good reason. It is competitively priced, easy to store and you can buy it in bulk. There is plenty of choice, with numerous big pet food brands jostling to win your custom. There is also some evidence that kibble with its crunchy texture may be better at keeping your cat's teeth clean and gums healthy than wet food. Dental health is important, both in its own right and because dental problems can impact other parts of the body. Studies have shown, for example, that improving a cat's dental health raises levels of immunoglobulin G, an important part of your cat's defence against bacteria and viruses. So dry cat food initially looks like a good option. But there are some downsides that you need to take into account.

Cats are susceptible to cystitis, an unpleasant and painful inflammation of the bladder. Idiopathic cystitis – that's cystitis for which there is no obvious or clear cause – has been linked to both stress and to diet in cats. There is a strong link between cats that are fed exclusively on dried food and an increased likelihood of suffering from cystitis. In one study, 59 per cent of cats fed on dried food suffered from cystitis compared with 19 per cent of cats in the general population.

Most experts recommend wet cat food for optimum health.

Another potential problem with dried food is keeping your cat adequately hydrated, and indeed this may be a contributing factor to the bladder problems identified in kibble-fed cats. Cats fed on dried food drink more than those fed on wet – however, when we take into account the water content of the food, their total water intake is actually less.

Bearing in mind these issues, many experts now recommend that all cats fed a commercial diet are fed predominantly on wet food, which will reduce your cat's risk of suffering from nasty bladder problems. Wet food includes the food you can buy in cans, pouches or trays. These are a little heavier and bulkier to store than kibble, but most come in portion-size containers and will keep for a long time. Wet food has the added benefit that most cats prefer it to kibble.

Because wet food has no abrasive action on your cat's teeth you need to think about how you are going to keep them clean. Some cat owners teach their cats to permit their teeth to be cleaned with a cat toothbrush and cat toothpaste. Others prefer to leave their cat's teeth alone as long as they seem in good condition. Some toys and chews claim to help keep a cat's teeth clean too. But there is another alternative that you might wish to consider, and that is an all-natural raw diet.

Raw feeding for cats

Raw feeding for both cats and dogs is becoming increasingly popular. It's also a controversial topic, with some veterinarians strongly against the practice, while others are promoting it. There are a great many claims made by raw feeding enthusiasts, including benefits to coat and skin, relief from allergies and even a stronger immune system. To date there is little in the way of firm evidence to support most of these claims, and perhaps the main benefit to most cats will be improved dental health.

As obligate carnivores, cats are ideally suited to a raw meat diet. But feeding raw isn't just a case of buying meat, cutting it up and putting it in a bowl. For a raw food diet to be a balanced one, it needs to contain a considerable amount of bone, and this bone content is one of the things that some vets worry about. Carnivores crush bones with their back teeth before swallowing them. Hard bones can break teeth and therefore it's important to find bones that are soft enough for your pet. The smaller your pet, the harder this is. And with cats, whose natural diet would be very small rodents and birds, getting the prey size small enough for their teeth to cope with the bones inside it can be challenging.

Because of these difficulties, and because not everyone enjoys preparing raw food for their pets, the pet food industry has stepped in to meet the demand and you can now buy a range of commercially prepared raw diets for cats. Raw meat of any kind contains pathogens that can be harmful if swallowed by humans so you'll need to handle it carefully. Pathogens have also been found in some kibbles too, so it's a good idea to keep pet food and bowls well away from areas where small children may come into contact with them.

Feeding a cat on a natural diet of raw meat flesh and organs is an achievable aim, but it isn't for everyone. If you are worried about bones, don't want to handle raw meat or are daunted by the idea of trying to provide a balanced diet, it might not suit you. If you do want to have a go at raw feeding, it is easier to start a kitten off this way than

Most cats won't let you forget that it's mealtime.

convert an older cat that is accustomed to commercial food. It's a good idea to get a comprehensive guide written by an expert. You'll find some references in the back of this book. On balance the sensible option for most families is to buy wet cat food in pouches, and to make sure a vet looks at their cat's teeth when they attend for vaccinations.

Cat feeding patterns

Because cats are solitary predators, they are only able to bring down prey much smaller than themselves, such as mice or birds. This means that it is natural for a cat to eat many small meals each day, rather than one large meal every 24 hours. This 'little and often' pattern of feeding is a set-up that your cat would naturally like to replicate in your home. If you have a cat which begs loudly for dinner every couple of hours like Oscar, you will be able to empathise with those that are tempted to simply plonk a giant bowl of dry food on the floor and leave the cat to top himself up at will. But that isn't always a good idea – some cats will overeat and become fat on this regime, and it can be problematic in homes where there is a family dog. So we need to look at the pros and cons of different feeding schedules.

Feeding schedules and quantities for kittens

Like most baby animals, kittens need feeding more often than adult cats, and their rate of growth is very rapid to begin with.

Billy's mealtimes and quantities at eight weeks:

7.30am	Quarter of a small can of grain-free kitten food	(25g/.88oz)
11am	Two heaped teaspoons of minced chicken breast	(30g/1oz)
2.30pm	Quarter of a small can of grain-free kitten food	(25g/.88oz)
7pm	Two heaped teaspoons of minced chicken breast	(30g/1oz)

Billy's mealtimes and quantities at 12 weeks:

8am	One small can of minced chicken breast	(75g/2.5oz)
1pm	One pouch of lamb chunks	(85g/3oz)
2.30pm	Half a tray of grain-free kitten food	(50g/1.75oz)

- Different kittens may need a little more or a little less. Remember that they have really tiny stomachs! You can be guided by the instructions on the tin, but start small and work up gradually with a new kitten or you may find they get diarrhoea.

- Most new kittens will need no more than 120 grams (4.25 ounces) of kitten food per day divided into four separate meals. You might also like to buy a small amount of freeze-dried meat treats to use for training.

Feeding schedules and quantities for adult cats

Non-breakable bowls mean older children can help with feeding.

Adult domestic cats are usually fed once or twice a day. Or at least their owners think they are. Morning and evening mealtimes make a convenient schedule for anyone out at work all day. And although this isn't a natural pattern for a cat, it can work well. With cats allowed outdoors, you may find that you are competing for your cat's attentions with other sources of food. This includes wild animals that your cat catches and (especially in areas with denser populations) the contents of the cat bowls in your neighbours' homes.

It is not uncommon for people to feed cats that are not their own. It is probably with the best of intentions, but this can cause problems for us as cat owners – especially when it comes to looking after our cat's weight, or monitoring health conditions that are impacted by diet.

There are a couple of alternatives to morning and evening feeds for adult cats. We've mentioned leaving food down all day so the cat can help himself, but as this is only suitable for dry food and in single pet homes, we don't recommend it. Another option is to feed your cat multiple times each day. This schedule has the advantage of matching your cat's natural feeding pattern, and it may also reduce a cat's inclination to roam. Billy is still fed four times a day as Pippa feels it helps to keep him from straying too far. If your family are all out at work during the day, you can still provide at least three meals every 24 hours by giving one meal before you leave for work in the morning, one when you get home from work in the evening, and one before you go to bed last thing at night. An alternative for providing multiple feeds for a cat is an automatic feeder with a timer on. Those with a pop-up lid (to keep the wet food moist and clean) are the best option. These are usually capable of delivering one or two meals.

What should cats drink?

Traditionally cats and milk go hand in hand. Rudyard Kipling's 'Cat Who Walked By Himself' bargained his mouse-catching skills and kindness to babies in exchange for warm white milk. And many stories with a cat include a 'saucer of milk'. Nowadays, more people are aware that milk can cause unpleasant reactions in some adult mammals, and that cow's milk is not an ideal food for most cats. According to a research report by pet food manufacturer Purina, intolerance to dairy products (including milk) is the second most common food allergen that has been identified in both dogs and cats.

But it's important for your cat's health that he remains well hydrated, so what should you provide for your cat in the form of liquid refreshment?

Even if your cat drinks very little, it's important to provide clean drinking water at all times. Have a couple of bowls dedicated to this purpose and put a clean one down each morning. Refill the bowl with fresh water before you go to bed at night. A couple of small studies have shown that cats may have a preference for running water, as on average they drank (slightly) more from a fountain than they did from a bowl. As always, the pet product manufacturers have caught on and you can now buy a range of pet water fountains. Before you empty your wallet, bear in mind some of the cats in the studies mentioned actually preferred the still water.

If you want to provide your cat with an occasional saucer of milk that's fine, but remember that you still need to provide drinking water. It's also important to recognise that you are adding calories to your cat's daily food allowance and to keep your eye out for any signs that milk is upsetting his stomach.

What goes in . . .

In conclusion, wet food is better for cats than dry and helps to avoid painful bladder problems. Throughout their lives cats prefer small frequent meals, but with the exception of small kittens most cats will do fine being fed morning and evening. If you can feed your adult cat more frequently that's a bonus, and may help to keep him closer to home. Always have a couple of bowls of fresh water available for your cat to drink.

11
Clean and Dry

What goes in to your cat must eventually come out again, and the other end of your cat's digestion is something we are going to look at in some detail in this chapter. For some families, house training simply isn't an issue. They provide the box, the cat uses it. But this is also a common area for people to get into difficulties. One of the main reasons for people to relinquish a cat to an animal shelter is behaviour problems, including soiling in the house. For that reason alone this is an important topic – let's find out how to make sure you get your cat clean and dry at home with as little fuss as possible.

Your first consideration when it comes to house training your new cat or kitten will be the litter box itself. If you are anything like us, you'd rather not have one at all. Let's face it, there isn't a room in your home that would look better because of one. However, with the exception of farm cats that live their entire lives outdoors, almost all domestic cats have to learn to use a litter box at some point in their lives. And for anyone with a new cat it's a non-negotiable reality. Your cat won't be able to go outdoors when they first move in with you, and if ever your cat is sick and needs medical treatment in the future, they could be kept indoors for days, weeks or even months. So it's best to bite the bullet and get good litter box habits established right from the start.

Litter box training

Happily, you don't have to explain to your cat what the litter box is for. Cats naturally like to dig a hole in soft soil to poop and pee in, and cat litter has a similar appeal. Provided the litter is the only 'diggable' substance in the room, it's where nearly all cats will head for bathroom purposes. It's a question of helping them to choose the diggable dish that you have set up for them, and removing the large pot plant in the corner of the room. You want to set your kitty up to win.

Put your litter box into an obvious corner of your cat's safe room. You can find tips on choosing a litter box in Chapter 7: Final Preparations. Remove flaps, doors, lids, etc., from the box if it has them (you can put them back later), and put a thick layer of cat litter in the bottom. The litter needs to be deep enough for the cat to be able to bury his waste in, about 3.5 to 5 centimetres (1 to 2 inches). Make sure it is easy to climb into, and that your cat can see the litter box from anywhere in the room. It's important to keep the box clean as most cats will look for an alternative if their own bathroom is dirty. You'll need to remove any obvious waste morning and evening and give the box a good scrub with detergent at least twice a week. Litter that your new cat is familiar with is best – if you want to change to a different type, mix it 50/50 with the old style of litter for a few days to maintain some continuity for your cat.

Avoiding litter box accidents

Sometimes things go wrong and litter box training never really gets established, or it breaks down for what can be a variety of reasons. We'll look at some of those in a moment. The chances are, you won't have problems if you follow a few basic rules. Cats are basically very clean animals provided you can meet these conditions for them.

For the best chance of litter box success your cat needs:

- **A plain open-topped litter box**
- **Familiar and accessible litter box location**
- **Enough litter to bury their waste in**
- **The litter box to be cleaned daily**
- **Round the clock access to the litter box**
- **A litter box for every cat in the home**
- **A spare litter box in another location in the house.**

We've looked at the first four, let's look at those last three now.

Round the clock access to the litter box is inevitable when your cat is confined to his safe room during those first few days. But once the cat is allowed to wander freely about the house it's more of an effort for him to make his way back to go to the toilet, and at some point someone will inadvertently close the door to the room with the litter box in it. Placing another litter box in another part of the house is a thoughtful concession to a new cat, especially if your home is large.

Although technically one litter box each should be fine, most experts recommend also having a spare in another area of the house. This gives the cat more choice of locations, and means that if they are put off approaching one for some reason there is an easily available alternative. To start with, make the new box the same style as the familiar box. Once your kitty is used to using them, you can try making changes. If your cat does have an accident, switch back to the old style of litter box before it becomes a habit.

If you have another cat, that extra box is essential. Not all cats who share a litter box will have accidents, but having enough litter boxes for all the cats in your house so that they don't have to share is important.

Not all cats will poop on the carpet if someone accidentally blocked them from getting at the litter box for an hour or two. Adult cats that are well established in the family home can usually wait several hours to toilet in an emergency. But in general it pays to set your pet up to win. If you want to avoid any accidents whatsoever, familiarity with and access to a choice of litter boxes is key.

Toilet troubleshooting

Sometimes the first sign that the cat is not using the litter box is when you discover a small parcel underneath an item of furniture or tucked away in the corner of a room. Or you may notice that the cat is wetting bed covers or furniture. Sometimes a cat will pee next to the litter box instead of inside it. Toileting issues, or what scientists like to call 'inappropriate eliminations', come in several guises. There are many possible reasons that your cat might start to use your bed as a bathroom, or spray urine up against the kitchen units with apparent reckless abandon. The one thing these issues all have in common is how upsetting they are for the human members of the family. It's important not to get caught up in blaming your cat. They don't want to upset you and your focus needs to be on figuring out underlying cause of the problem.

It's important to distinguish between elimination for the purpose of emptying the bowels or bladder, and 'marking' which involves the cat deliberately peeing a small amount of urine up against a wall or vertical surface in order to leave

Cats are naturally clean, but there are ways to help avoid problems.

in order to leave a prominent scent mark in the home. These are two different behaviours and need to be discussed separately. Marking, or deliberately spraying urine, is a behavioural problem that won't affect the majority of cat owners. If you are unfortunate enough to have a cat that starts 'marking' at home, you'll find help and information in Chapter 16: Cats Behaving Badly. We'll deal with basic toilet training problems here.

Using the wrong bathroom

Scent marking aside, there are a number of reasons that cats may pee and poop inappropriately in the home. Working out the cause can help you to identify potential solutions, so let's take a look at some of these. They include:

- Ill health
- Old age
- Stress/fear
- Unfamiliarity with the litter box
- Having to share a litter box
- Infrequent litter box cleaning.

As an immediate first step, make sure that anywhere your cat has eliminated that is not inside the litter box is very thoroughly cleaned. Cats have an excellent sense of smell and just the smallest trace of odour from the accident may encourage the cat to repeat the mistake. Swab the area thoroughly with warm water and detergent, and then specialist pet urine cleaners will do a good job on the smell. Next we need to identify the cause of the accident.

Health problems

This is important to look into, especially in a cat that was previously clean. Bladder infections are common in cats and can result in your cat wetting his bed or the furniture. A check-up with the vet will help to rule out this kind of problem and is an essential first step when any previously clean cat starts wetting in the home.

Old age

Sometimes cats become incontinent when they get old. This isn't inevitable but it does happen. The important thing to know is that there are effective treatments available. We'll take a look at these in more detail in Chapter 20: Your Senior Cat, but it makes sense to have your cat examined by the vet if his toilet training habits have deteriorated, so that any underlying health issues can be addressed.

Stress

Just as health problems can cause cats to urinate inappropriately, so can stress. Like many humans, cats aren't big fans of change. Moving house, the birth of a baby or the arrival of a new puppy can change the atmosphere in the home. Toileting accidents when the family is already under stress are common and often resolve when things settle down. Some experts recommend feline pheromone diffusers for these situations – they release maternal pheromones that cats recognise and that may help soothe some cats when they are feeling anxious. You can buy ones that plug into an electric socket.

Unfamiliarity with the box

If you find your cat stops using the box after it's replaced with a shiny new version, then sadly it might be time to switch back to the old style. If you switched to a different type of litter around the time that the trouble started you may need to switch back. If your cat is not using the litter box and he never has, replicate the scenario we discussed for a new cat. Create a safe room with a litter box in a really obvious place, making sure it is one that is easy for him to access, so with no roof or door, and that it contains litter that doesn't have an off-putting odour. Make sure that there isn't anywhere more appealing where the cat can choose to poop or pee, and restrict the cat to this room until he is regularly using the box provided. When this succeeds, gradually open up the rest of the house, room by room, only adding each new area when they have been clean and dry for a week in the previous one.

Having to share a litter box

Cats don't generally like sharing resources, and that includes their toilet. If you have two cats you should have at least two litter boxes, preferably a fair distance away from each other. Even if your cat has shared happily before, if they begin to eliminate in inappropriate places, an extra litter box may solve the problem.

Litter box hygiene

Many cats are very fussy about bathroom hygiene. Some won't consider a box that isn't well attended, and cleaning the box out more regularly can improve their enthusiasm for using it. The minimum we would recommend is twice a day, morning and evening, with extra scoops in between if you notice that they have had a bowel movement. The box itself should be completely cleaned with pet safe spray at least twice a week.

Although peeing and pooing outside of the litter box when your cat needs the toilet is distressing, it's a problem that can often be tackled through the methods above. And if your cat eventually has outdoor access, you may be able to dispense with litter boxes in your home altogether, as Lucy and Pippa have both done.

Leaving the litter box behind

If you are dreaming of the day when you can banish the last litter box from your home, you are not alone. While some cat owners will keep their pet indoors throughout their life, many cats have at least some access to the outdoors. Their owners expect to be able to ditch the litter box at that point. Billy and Oscar no longer have litter boxes indoors, and most established adult cats with round-the-clock access to the garden won't need one either. But it is important to make the transition carefully in order to avoid accidents. Oscar and Billy both have the freedom to come and go as they please, at any hour of the day. And even though their transition was similarly timed at around seven months of age, the process for each was different. You'll need to adapt your own transition to suit your cat, but here are the two different methods we used.

Billy had two litter boxes available to him. One downstairs in Pippa's office – which had been his safe room – and one upstairs in the family bathroom, which he used less frequently. When Billy started to go outdoors he quite rapidly stopped using his litter boxes. Within days he had abandoned them altogether, and after leaving it there for a week to make sure he didn't want to revisit it, Pippa was able to remove the downstairs box (his favourite). He never used the upstairs one again, and after another couple of weeks she removed that too. Super simple!

However, things did not go that way for Oscar. Although he loved going outdoors to play, hunt and visit all the neighbours' cats' food bowls, he was still more than happy to return home to go to the toilet. This wasn't a problem for a while, but when he was around a year old, Lucy became pregnant and decided that she'd rather avoid the risk of toxoplasmosis that cat faeces have been associated with.

In order to help Oscar to stop using his box the family gradually moved it towards the back door. Just a few inches a day, until it was beside the back door. When it had sat there for a couple of days they put it outside, and Oscar stopped using it completely. This transition worked well for him, but it was helped by the fact that the box was kept near the back door beforehand, so it was only a matter of a few feet for it to leave the house. Once it was outdoors, Oscar decided he'd rather go in the flowerbed than the litter anyway.

If you want to help your cat transition in this manner then take it slowly, and if they make a mistake then move the box back to the area where it was before the mistake was made and move even more gradually the next time. Just like you did when setting the box up in the beginning, you want to set your cat up to win.

Set your cat up to win

Toileting problems are a big deal and we want to do everything we can to avoid them cropping up. They are one of the main reasons that cats are relinquished at animal shelters. It's therefore really important that they are avoided where possible, and treated fast and effectively when they occur. If for any reason you ever have to part with your cat, or your cat has to be rehomed, good litter box habits will help to ensure he finds a loving new family.

Litter box use is as much about good management as it is about training. If you follow the tips above you are unlikely to have too much trouble getting your cat clean and dry and keeping him that way. Don't hesitate to contact your vet if you are struggling; all vets are used to dealing with inappropriate elimination in cats and there are drugs that can help in some cases. Hopefully your cat, like most, won't have toileting issues. And if they do, they will be short lived and easily resolved.

When the time comes, if you decide to allow your cat to venture out into the wide world, then you may be able to put life with a litter box behind you.

12

Indoors to Outdoors

L etting your cat go free is a big decision and one that many of us worry about. Whether or not to take the plunge and how to do it as safely as possible is the topic of this chapter. According to a recent study, over 90 per cent of UK cats have daily outdoor access, but in other parts of the world there is a growing trend for owners to keep their cats confined to the house for the entirety of their lives. In the USA it is estimated that around 50–60 per cent of cats live permanently indoors. The pressure to keep cats confined is greatest in regions like Australasia, where cats are seen as a huge threat to the indigenous wildlife. We will look at some of the factors that might influence this trend.

Indoor vs outdoor – the great debate

Cats are fairly unique when it comes to life as a pet. They are domesticated, and yet they still appear to be very much a wild animal in terms of their ability to live independently from us. There will always be a certain amount of compromise involved in keeping a highly efficient predator in our homes. If they were given the choice, cats would spend some of their day hunting and eating small meals of tiny prey animals, some of the day sleeping in secluded spots and the rest begging at the larder door or purring in your lap. A cat with his own back door can simply go out when he feels the urge and arrive back when he hears the car pull into the drive or our feet stomping up the path. Studies show that there may be health benefits to cats in having the freedom to roam and hunt. Yet there are clearly risks in our modern world in allowing a small and distractible animal to go where he pleases.

While we feel that the two sides to this debate are equally valid, and although Oscar was originally intended to be an indoor cat, we now both allow our cats the freedom to roam. Deciding whether to let your cat experience an independent outdoor life is one of the biggest choices that a new cat owner has to make, and there are a number of vocal proponents on both sides of the debate. Let's take a closer look at the arguments.

There may be health benefits to cats in having the freedom to roam and explore.

The impact of cats on wildlife

We all know that cats are great hunters. If your cat is allowed to roam free outdoors he will kill small animals and birds. If you cannot bear the thought of that happening, you should probably have an indoor cat. However, if it isn't the practical side of dealing with prey animals that concerns you as much as the ethical debate, it's important to look at the bigger picture and to examine the evidence. Do cats actually cause an environmental problem? Are cats capable of decimating the wild bird population for example, or have we overestimated their impact? Unfortunately, this is a topic on which not all experts agree, and the evidence is at times conflicting.

A study in Western Australia, where cats are considered to be a serious threat to small marsupials, found that there were just as many different species of wild animals in areas where cats were not restricted as there were in cat restriction areas. And though the total numbers of wild animals was slightly higher in areas with fewer cats, the main influence on numbers was the amount of vegetation present. In the UK, the Royal Society for the Protection of Birds have looked at the evidence and seem unconvinced that cats are harmful to our wild bird populations. That's despite the fact that they estimate cats are responsible for killing around 55 million birds each year, mostly song birds – i.e. birds that we see in our gardens. The RSPB points out that the evidence suggests cats kill weak or sick birds. And that those bird species most at risk from declining populations, such as skylarks, don't normally come into contact with cats.

A US study published in *Nature Communications* in 2013 came to a very different conclusion. It describes domestic cats as probably 'the single greatest source of anthropogenic mortality for US birds and mammals', and in 2016 the book *Cat Wars* was published in America, which called for the widespread extermination of outdoor cats. Supporters of cat eradication tend to focus on the numbers of animals caught and killed by cats, but there is a bigger picture. To understand that we need to consider how predators in general affect their prey.

Biologically, predation is not necessarily a bad thing. In fact it can actually be beneficial. Predators are more successful in catching and killing other animals when those animals are weak or disabled in some way. If predator numbers are not too high, the effect of predation can be to strengthen the population by eliminating the weaker individuals from the gene pool. We also know that predators and their prey are capable of living in balance together, as they do in many parts of the world. But are cat populations now so high that they are out of balance with the animals that they prey on? It seems that the jury is still out on this question.

Obviously we should not be complacent about the impact of our cats on local wildlife, and the situation needs to be monitored, and reviewed regularly as fresh evidence comes to light. It makes sense too to consider keeping your cat indoors if you live within or adjacent to an area that is known to be home to a rare or threatened species of bird vulnerable to predation by cats.

In addition to the potential impact of your cat on the environment, the choice you make over your cat's freedom has the potential to impact on your cat's health and welfare too. It seems fairly obvious that the freedom to roam carries risks, yet many people are unaware that keeping a cat indoors may carry risks of its own. Let's look at the pros and cons to your cat of being given the freedom to roam.

The risks to your cat of going outdoors

One of the potential dangers for outdoor cats is attacks by other animals. In the USA mammalian predators such as coyotes, large birds of prey, and in some areas large reptiles, all pose a threat to cats. In the UK we don't have big predators any more. While people worry that foxes might pose a threat, most experts doubt that foxes will attack an adult cat. In fact there is no hard evidence that foxes attack cats at all. So for all intents and purposes the cat is pretty much the top of the tree when it comes to hunting. Arguably dogs are a potential threat, but most cats can outrun and outmanoeuvre most dogs, and here in Britain stray or roaming dogs are no longer common. All in all, the risk to a healthy adult cat of being injured or killed by other animals is fairly low.

Fighting with other cats is however an occasional hazard, and most cats get the odd bite or scratch at some point in their lives, usually when there's a new cat on the street. This is rarely serious but may need attention from a vet. Another concern for outdoor cat owners around the world is violence from humans.

Perhaps the main risk unique to outdoor cats in densely populated areas is traffic. In urban or suburban areas around the world, letting your cat navigate their way around streets or lanes can feel rather scary, with good reason. In a study of 4,000 cats in the UK the most common cause of death to cats was trauma, at around 12 per cent of cases. Of this about half of deaths were assumed to be traffic related. This figure differed when you broke it down into age categories. For example, cats under five years old were most likely to have a cause of death related to traffic, infections or respiratory disorders. Over five years kidney problems, general illness and tumours were key candidates. We could assume that this means cats over five years old have learned how to relatively safely navigate roads and are therefore at less risk. What we know for sure from that study is that on average cats appear to live in general for 14 years, but the peak times for death were at around one year and 16 years old. So if you do decide to let your young cat out, the first five years are the most risky, and the first year is probably the riskiest of all.

Of course, we cannot tell you whether or not your cat will survive outdoors or be hit by a car, only that cats appear to be less at risk as they get older. Only you can decide if that is a level of risk you are prepared to take. And before you make that decision, it makes sense to look at the benefits to your cat of going outdoors

The benefits to your cat of going outdoors

The mental stimulation and physical exercise that cats get from hunting and exploring outdoors are extremely hard to replicate in the home. In the space of a morning, Billy or Oscar may climb up a seven-foot gate several times, balance along the top of the fence for twenty yards, leap across a five-foot gap onto a garage roof, run eighty yards up the garden and back, stalk a mouse and chase a woodpigeon. And while it's true that cats spend a great deal of the day sleeping, when they are active, they are very active indeed. Unlike most dogs, most indoor cats don't get taken for walks, and tend to have reduced opportunities for running, jumping, climbing and exploring. Some studies have linked health conditions such as cystitis with confinement, others have concluded that owners of indoor cats are simply more likely to notice these problems. But we do know that cats that lack a rich and stimulating environment can become bored and stressed, and may become obese or display undesirable behaviours in the home.

Most of those who allow their cats outdoors do so because they believe that their outdoor cat has a better quality of life than a cat that spends its days within four walls. This is something that is very hard to quantify, define or defend. Sometimes you just have to go with your gut feeling. You may also want to consider the benefits of an outdoor cat to the family as a whole.

The great outdoors gives your cat plenty of space to stretch his legs.

The benefits to you of having an outdoor cat

The lack of litter box in the home is a bonus for outdoor cat owners. Cleaning out a litter box is not just an unpleasant chore, it is also a health risk to humans who are vulnerable to infection, and a frequent source of conflict in homes with dogs who for some reason love to eat cat poop! The litter box issue will be particularly relevant to you if your dog is small enough to get through cat doors and baby gates, or if you are pregnant and worried about the risk of toxoplasmosis from coming into contact with faeces.

Indoor cats can go 'stir crazy' at times. And many owners, Lucy included, reverse a decision to keep their cat indoors when the cat's activity levels peak at around five to six months old. Problems that arise in indoor cats through a lack of mental stimulation and exercise can be minimised by what behaviourists call environmental enrichment. We'll look at those next, but it's important to recognise that they do demand some time and effort on the part of the cat owner. The owner of an outdoor cat won't need to worry about entertaining their pet once they have outgrown the kitten stage. If you decide to keep your cat indoors permanently, you'll find tips and ideas for keeping him entertained in Chapter 16: Cats Behaving Badly.

Making your choice

Both Billy and Oscar are outdoor cats. They each have a cat flap in their back door which allows them to come and go as they please. Since kittenhood the only times Oscar and Billy have been prevented from going outside are Bonfire Night and New Year's Eve, due to the loud scary fireworks, and when they have been kept in for medical reasons – after being neutered for example, or in Oscar's case after being wounded in a fight. A fight which, it must be pointed out, would have never occurred had he not had access to the outside world.

It is our personal belief that outdoor cats in relatively safe suburban or rural areas have a wonderful quality of life and that this benefit outweighs the risks involved. But this doesn't mean that we are right. You need to decide what you are comfortable with, and look at the pros and cons of your particular home set-up and surrounding environment. And consider how you would feel if the worst were to happen to your cat on his trips outdoors. Only you can know what is the right choice for you and your cat. If you do decide to give your cat his freedom, it's important to recognise that the risks are real and do what you can to minimise them.

Outdoor cats find their own entertainment and new places to relax.

Keeping your outdoor cat safe

First steps outdoors

When you make the decision to let your cat roam, it's important to take steps to keep him as safe as possible. Those first few trips outdoors are a particularly vulnerable time for any cat, and it's a good idea to keep them brief to begin with. The best way to achieve this is to only let your cat outside just before mealtime.

Microchipping

If your cat gets lost, you can increase the likelihood of him being returned to you by having him microchipped. We highly recommend that you also microchip your cat or kitten if they are even intended to stay indoors. An indoor cat that escapes is not going to be as familiar with his local environment, and a microchip ensures that you will get him back as quickly as possible. It also means that if something devastating were to happen and your cat was injured while outside the home, a vet would be able to identify him and contact you.

A collar with a bell may help to warn birds that your cat is approaching.

The pros and cons of cat collars

Another less permanent way to identify your cat is with a collar. While collars can be removed and discarded, they can enable a kind person to contact you if they find your cat. There is another benefit to a collar, which Lucy has personally seen with her outdoor cat Oscar. Perhaps the biggest risk to outdoor cats is theft by neighbours, and friendly cats are particularly vulnerable. In most cases the neighbour is probably not intending to permanently deprive the cat owner of their pet, but what starts as offering the occasional treat or saucer of milk to a visiting cat can end with that cat moving in. At best, if a neighbour is feeding him you are likely to end up with an overweight cat. This is what happened to Oscar. After several months of struggling to keep the weight off him, Lucy gave him a nice new collar with 'DO NOT FEED' printed repeatedly all around its length. Oscar regained his waistline within a week or two.

Not every cat will accept a collar, and some owners worry about the risk of them getting tangled up in the undergrowth. You can buy collars with a break section that snaps if the cat gets caught up by it. Unfortunately some cats learn to get these off by putting a paw inside and pulling till the break strip gives way. Billy did this and is a great climber so he no longer wears a collar, but Pippa uses other strategies to reduce his risk of accident or injury outdoors by keeping him close to home.

Frequent feeding

The further your cat goes from home the greater the risk of him getting lost or coming to harm. If your cat spends much of his day in your garden he should be safer than a cat who is out crossing roads or visiting neighbours. One way to keep a cat near to home is to feed him more frequently. Many adult cats are only fed twice a day, and a lot can happen in twelve hours. If you feed your cat four to six times a day, not only is this a more natural feeding pattern for a cat, but they will be less tempted to wander further afield.

Recall

We strongly recommend that you train your cat to come home when you whistle or call him. We'll be looking at teaching this and other useful skills together with some entertaining tricks, in the next chapter.

Keeping your indoor cat happy

Living indoors will protect your cat from attacks by dogs or humans and from road traffic accidents. Whether or not the risks of these potential disasters have been overstated, and to what extent they apply to you and your cat, will depend partly on where you live.

However, life indoors may also expose your cat to some risks. These risks include behavioural problems and obesity, and possibly other health issues too, related to lack of exercise and mental stimulation. These risks can be mitigated to some extent if you have the space and funds to provide a cat wheel or a large outdoor enclosure. Cats don't just like to hunt, they need to, so you must also engage your cat in play that mimics hunting.

Training is both fun and rewarding. If you teach your cat some simple tricks, not only will you be enriching his life you'll also help to build a strong bond of friendship between you.

13
Training and Tricks

Tricks are a great way to keep your cat entertained on a rainy day.

It's common to hear people say that their cat is far too clever or too independent to be trained. And also common to hear that cats are stupid and can't be trained like dogs. In fact cats are both intelligent and trainable. And their independence, though challenging in some respects, is not an absolute barrier to training. There are many good reasons to train your cat. It's a great way to spend time together, it helps to build a bond between you and can also make your cat's life easier. A visit to the vet, for example, will be more relaxing if you can train your cat to climb into his carrier on cue and to allow anyone to open his mouth, inspect his teeth or examine his paws.

Modern training techniques are not just fun for your pets, they are enjoyable for you too. Pet training methods have changed immensely in the last decade, and no longer involve the use of force. Instead, your pet will think that they are playing a very rewarding game. This is great news for cat people, because as you are probably aware trying to *force* a cat to do anything is fraught with difficulty.

In this chapter we'll introduce the simple tools you'll need to train your cat, look at how to deal with some of the challenges you are likely to meet in cat training and give you a few examples to get you started. Animal training isn't rocket science, but if you want to succeed before your cat gets bored and wanders off, it helps to have an understanding of the basic principles involved. We'll begin by looking at how cats learn new behaviours and how you can use that knowledge to get your cat to play the training game.

How cats learn

In nature, learning is all about consequences. If something your cat does is followed by a great consequence, they'll repeat it. If something they do is followed by an unpleasant consequence they likely won't repeat it. In training the principle is exactly the same. In the past animal trainers used unpleasant consequences such as a squirt of water, or even a slap, to punish undesirable behaviour, and praise or treats to reinforce (make it happen again) behaviour that they liked.

Modern animal trainers have discovered that, on the whole, animals learn much quicker when we remove the unpleasant consequences side of the equation and simply reinforce desirable behaviours. Not only do animals learn faster this way, but unwanted side effects of punishment (including aggression, impaired learning and owner avoidance) are neatly side-stepped.

There are some provisos to this modern system. The first is that in order to reinforce behaviours the rewards must be highly desirable to the cat. The second is that the reinforcement must happen at the same time or very shortly after the behaviour took place.

How cat training works

It's no good rewarding a cat for jumping through a hoop five minutes after it did so. Or even after two minutes. The reinforcement has to come immediately, as the animal completes the jump. So, to train your cat, not only going you are to provide reinforcement for great behaviour you are going to have to provide that reinforcement *without delay*. It can be challenging at times to reinforce behaviour promptly, especially if your cat isn't close by. So we use a clicker to mark the moment that the cat does the thing you wanted him to do.

What is a clicker for?

The clicker is an event marker. Every click is followed by a tiny treat. The cat soon learns that each click predicts a treat, and from that moment the click acts as a reinforcer, and buys you a moment or two in which to deliver a treat to your cat. Because the click is so precise, we can accurately mark very specific behaviours such as a higher wave or a paw, or any other small movement or fleeting action completed by the cat.

What do I use for rewards?

It's important to remember that the cat decides what is a great reward and what isn't. Not you. Cats are all individuals, and what motivates them will differ from one to the other. Oscar would do just about anything for a tiny bit of cheese, but only for around four minute intervals. After that he will be out and about again. Billy loves Dreamies, a commercial cat treat, and Pippa has found them very useful reinforcers in his training. Training treats must also be very tiny, or your cat will soon be full and will wander off for a nap just as you are starting to have fun. If you do a lot of training you'll find it helpful to wear a treat bag attached to a belt and to keep several small pots of treats handy. Of course, you will need to subtract the food you use in training from your cat's daily food allowance.

Cats enjoy training provided there is plenty of motivation.

Understanding cues

Your aim in pet training is to be able to give a signal and have your cat make the right response. Trainers call these signals 'cues' rather than commands, because it aims to trigger a response in an animal rather than demand one. The end result should be the same, a cat that responds reliably to a particular cue with a specific action. A cue can be a hand signal, a whistle or a word. If you want to teach your cat to recall from any distance we suggest you buy a dog whistle, which is a more consistent cue, and carries much further than the human voice.

To teach your cat the meaning of your cue, simply pair the cue repeatedly with the action that you want the cat to carry out. So, with recall, you might pair a whistle or your cat's name with the act of running towards you. And for a high five you might use the cue of your own raised hand to get your cat to give you a raised paw in return. After many pairings the association between the cue and the response will become so strong that, when you give the cue, the cat will respond without thinking.

Obviously, you can't pair a cue with an action unless you can get your cat to carry out the action in the first place. And that is what your first training sessions are for.

Teaching a cat to carry out an action

To train your cat, you'll decide what action you want him to carry out. Then you'll use one of three different techniques to get that action and reinforce it. Those three techniques are:

- Capturing
- Luring
- Shaping.

Once your cat is carrying out the action you'll be able to add a cue. But the action needs to come first.

Capturing

With your clicker and treats ready, watch your cat closely until he does what you want him to do. Immediately CLICK and throw the cat a tiny TREAT (C&T). Capturing is a bit like taking a snapshot of an event. But it does require that the cat carries out the action in the first place. This is fine if the action is something that the cat does a lot. But most times you'll need some extra help from one of those other two training techniques.

Luring

You may need to use a lure to get the action you want to begin with. For example, to get your cat to sit up on his back legs with front paws in the air you can hold a treat over his head just out of reach. As soon as both front paws leave the ground click and throw a treat with the other hand. Luring should always be a temporary stop-gap, so replace the lure as soon as possible with a signal. In this case lure the cat into the begging position with a treat two or three times, then show the cat your empty hand and make a fake luring moving with it.

He'll most likely follow your hand into the position you want even though he knows it's empty, then C&T with the other hand as before. You have now replaced the lure with a hand signal! You may have to lure a couple or three times more before you can lose the lure completely.

Shaping

Another useful and very powerful technique is called shaping. It involves clicking and treating your cat for an approximation of the behaviour you want, or a step towards it, and then gradually moving the goalposts by delaying the click and waiting for something better. Shaping is often used to teach animals tricks. Let's look at an example.

Teaching tricks

Choose a shallow box and place it on the floor. Start by click and treating the cat for simply touching the box. With shaping you need to begin with the nearest approximation to the final behaviour that is available to you. In some cases this can be as simple as a look or glance in the right direction. Throw the treat away from the box after you click, to give the cat a chance to come back for another go. Your aim is to C&T your cat for putting a paw in a box, then delay the click until he puts two paws in the box and finally all four paws. Don't move the goalpost until the cat is succeeding nine out of every ten times at the previous goalpost. Once your cat is able to carry out the action(s) that you are looking for, and willingly jumps into the box when you place it on the floor, you can add a cue.

The example above is a trick called Four Paws In A Box and it's a popular one for people just starting out in dog training. Cats can be taught to entertain us in exactly the same way. In some respects the cat is more versatile, because their body is better adapted for balancing and bending, and because they are more willing to use their paws. Another simple trick is a High Five. This can be taught more quickly if you start with a lure. Pin a treat to the palm of your hand with your thumb, and hold your clicker in the other hand. Hold your hand just out of reach of the cat. C&T any movement of his paw towards it. Repeat two or three times then lose the lure. Shape until you get a nice high paw touch to your palm. In this way your cat can be taught any action that is comfortably within his physical capabilities.

Cat training challenges

With kittens, or cats that are not allowed outdoors, controlling your cat's access to 'competing reinforcers' is relatively simple. A competing reinforcer is anything else that your cat might enjoy, from stealing food from your toddler's plate to chasing the toy your five-year-old is dragging across the floor. What your cat often wants is food, and you have it, so you can use food as a reward in a room where there are no other distractions.

Once a cat is allowed his freedom, you will have to compete with the reinforcers provided by the outside world. Whether this is the thrill of hunting mice or the pleasure of eating your next-door neighbour's cat's dinner. Competing reinforcers are much more difficult to control with cats than with dogs, simply because most cats can leave whenever they please. For this reason, many highly trained cats are cats that live indoors and are not permitted to go outside.

That doesn't mean you cannot train a cat that is allowed out. You can, but you may need to be more modest in your ambitions.

Into a carrier on command

Even more rewarding than trick training is time spent teaching your cat life skills that will help him cope with stressful events and activities. Some of these skills are best achieved with a clicker, but in other cases, such as the recall, you won't need to use an event marker at all.

Training your cat to go into his carrier on a cue from you is a great way to have fun and to make your cat's life less stressful. No more wrestling with him when you need to go to the vet.

Again this uses shaping. To begin with you may need to click and treat your cat for simply looking at the carrier. Then for taking a step towards it, then for putting a paw inside, and so on. Throw the treat away from the carrier so that the cat has to actively turn back towards it again in order to get another treat. Once you have shaped your cat to go into the crate you can add a cue, such as 'Crate time!' or 'Into bed'. Start leaving a tiny treat in the crate at different times of the day, then say the cue when your cat is near the crate – he will naturally look inside and is rewarded by the treat. Over time, you can gradually increase the distance between the cat and the crate before giving your cue.

Using a cat flap

Many of us fit a cat flap into our homes, and you can help your cat to learn to use his more quickly. It's best to let your cat explore the outside world a little before teaching him to use his own door. Your cat needs to be familiar with what is on both sides of the flap. When you decide it's time to teach your cat to use his door, get a handful of tasty cat treats. Sit on the floor beside the door and give him a treat or two to really get his attention. Then with your other hand push the flap open, and allow him to follow the treat in your first hand so that you give him a treat in the entrance. At this point some cats will simply climb straight through, but others will be more cautious.

Let the cat see that the flap is open and hold a treat in the opening. When he has confidently taken it, hold it a little further through so that he needs to have a paw in the gap before he can reach it. Increase in tiny increments until he is confident in moving himself through the gap. This process is made easier if you have a friend or family member willing to sit at the other side with more treats in their hands. You can then get your cat to move back and forward a few times before you start to close the flap with your hand, meaning that to get the treat he needs to push just a little to get through. You can change the speed of the process depending upon your kitty's confidence in the game.

Teaching your cat to come when called

We recommend that all outdoor cat owners train their cat to come when they are called. Fortunately, it's easier than you might think. The time to get this training started is those early days when your cat or kitten is still shut indoors. At this point you are the only potential food source.

Step 1: Choose a cue

Choose the cue you want your cat to come back to. This will usually be their name, but you can choose anything you like. From a word to a bell or a whistle. If you live in the countryside, where your cat is more likely to wander long distances, a whistle might be preferable to yelling across the fields. As far as your cat and his training goes, it doesn't matter what cue you choose, as long as it's pretty consistent.

Step 2: Stop calling your cat

Don't use the cue you have chosen to call your cat for his dinner (or to call him for any other reason yet). We don't want the cue to be associated with NOT coming to you. If your cat ignores his name choose a different cue.

Step 3: Call while the cat eats

Break your cat's daily food ration into as many small portions as you can. To begin with start to give your recall cue while your cat is eating. The idea is to build a strong association between food and the cue. Do this many times a day for several days.

Step 4: Call while the cat moves towards you

Remember not to call the cat! Start preparing his food, attract his attention by tapping the bowl or clapping your hands, but don't use the cue until your cat starts to move towards you. NOW you can call him! Keep calling all the way until he reaches you. And feed.

Step 5: Strengthen your signal

Doing this over and over, many times a day, creates a very strong link between being fed when hungry and the sound of the recall cue. So strong that one day you'll be able to call your cat from a long way away and he will come running when he hears your signal.

Step 6: Maintain the response

The key to maintaining a great response to your cue is to rarely test it, never punish it and frequently reinforce it. Testing is when you call your cat when he is asleep, out of your sight, busy or otherwise distracted. There is never any guarantee that a test will result in a response. But the less you test and the more you strengthen the association between eating and your cue, the better the chance of a test getting the right result.

Punishing is when responding to the recall is accompanied by an unpleasant experience. One common mistake with recall is to inadvertently punish it. Be warned that if you recall your cat and then give him an unpleasant experience (such as a trip to the vet or a bath) you will drastically weaken your cue.

Teaching your cat to tolerate handling

Many cats prefer not to be handled. They may be happy to have their cheeks rubbed or head stroked, but dislike having their flanks, belly and legs touched. Yet at some point in every cat's life they are likely to need to be examined by their owner or a vet, and all cats benefit from being taught to accept being touched on various parts of their body without having a major meltdown.

You can teach your cat to tolerate being handled by associating handling with food or other rewards. For a while, Billy decided he didn't want to be picked up and took to squirming and even placing his teeth on the hands of anyone that attempted to lift him off the ground. We taught Billy that being picked up by anyone was always associated with the arrival of a tasty treat. This meant involving every visitor to the house and persuading them to lift up the cat and give him a treat. Close family members got the exercise started by lifting Billy's front end very briefly and treating him every time, then gradually building up to carrying him around for longer periods. His aversion to being picked up is now cured and the worst outcome for anyone that does so is having Billy rifling through their pockets for food.

But what about the cat that won't even let you touch him, never mind lift his feet off the ground for a second or two? Well with animal training you have to begin with what you are offered. If your cat won't let you slip your hands under his belly to lift him, will he let you touch his head? If so start there. Treat every time you touch his head until he is happy with that.

When your cat is comfortable with his head being touched, work your way further back until you can stroke his shoulders, then touch him lower down and lower down (always briefly to start with) until you can slip your hands under the cat's belly and press upwards for a moment.

Gradually increase the pressure of your touches and their duration. Breaking off repeatedly to treat. Train when your cat is hungry and stop before he loses enthusiasm for the treats.

From pressing up under your cat's belly just behind his front legs you can progress to lifting him off the ground, and then to lifting him up entirely. Remembering to touch and treat, touch and treat.

The same process can be applied to any part of your cat's body. Spend a few minutes on this before every meal until you can lift and hold each of your cat's paws, look in his ears and open his mouth to view his teeth. This simple process will make for a much happier cat next time the vet wants to examine him.

Bonding with your cat

Training a cat is a lot of fun. When you are shaping behaviours, just remember not to move the goalposts until the cat has figured out what you want at the previous level. Proceed in tiny increments and don't be afraid to go back a step if you are not succeeding. Pick attractive food rewards, train when there are no distractions around and as often as you can.

Known as positive reinforcement training, the techniques described in this chapter are entirely force free and are suitable for cats of any age. Even tiny kittens can be taught using food rewards in this way. Positive reinforcement training is a great way of bonding with your cat because it creates an association between you and the rewards you are providing.

14

Bonding and Behaviour

Communication lies at the heart of friendship and one of the main aims of this book is to help you make friends with your cat. Achieving a bond and finding common ground is a relatively simple matter when both parties are attempting to speak the same language. When the individuals concerned belong to two different species, there can be misunderstandings. For the most part we get along pretty well with our independent feline friends and have managed to cross that language barrier in several different ways, but there is still room for improvement. That's what this chapter is all about.

Cats have two key ways of 'talking' to one another. One is with scent and the other is with body language. And while vocalisations do occur in cat to cat interactions, cats generally miaow in order to communicate with people.

Cats leave scent marks on objects in their home territory in a number of ways. By rubbing the sides of their face on the surfaces around them, by spraying urine and even by scratching with their claws, which leaves behind traces of scent from the pads in their feet. Scratching also leaves a visual signal that other cats may be able to interpret.

Cats don't just rub themselves against surfaces and other animals to put down scent. They also rub themselves to pick up the scent of other cats or creatures that they want to be associated with. Cats will also lick themselves when you have stroked them. Not to remove your scent, but to taste it! These actions all help to deepen the bond between you. The scent-marking actions that you are most likely to see in your cat on a daily basis are head bumping and body rubbing. Let's look a bit closer at those.

Head bumps and body rubs

If you examine the fur just in front of your cat's ears, you'll see that it is much sparser than the fur on the rest of his face. This area is covered with special glands

*The hair is thin in front of a cat's ears to help them
deposit scent when they rub with their heads.*

that produce oil rich in pheromones – chemical signals that many animals use
to identify, attract and deter others. When your cat arches his neck, dips his chin
down and bumps or rubs the top of his head on you, his intention is to smear
this oil on your skin and clothes so that you smell just like him. You'll also notice

your cat rubbing the side of his face and his mouth on you. That's because there are more of these glands in his cheeks and lips. There are glands in his tail too, and as he weaves in and out of your legs, his tail brushes against your clothes leaving a trail of scent on them. It's no coincidence that the area of the body that cats are most comfortable having touched are those areas that are densely covered in these glands. The more you stroke your cat's face and head, the more you spread his scent over your hands and body, marking you out as a privileged member of his inner social circle.

Although we have identified the chemical components of some of the odours that cats secrete and deposit around them, the exact meaning of these communications are not fully understood, and most are indistinguishable to the average human. Whether or not your cat intends these scent messages for you, the chances are you won't be able to read them. But body language is a different matter and you can definitely learn to read the shapes that cats throw. Cat tail language is one of the simplest cat signals to interpret.

Cat tail language

Your cat's tail has a very interesting structure. It contains a column of over a dozen bones wrapped in a tube of powerful muscles and covered in a beautiful sleeve of dense fur. Cats have considerable control over what their tail does. They can raise it aloft with the bones stacked on top of one another, tilt it to either side or trail it behind them. They can also quiver the whole tail or just the very tip. Every cat uses their tail for balancing, but it is also a powerful tool for communicating both with their adopted families and with other cats. Most of us know that, unlike dogs, a wagging or swishing tail in a cat indicates anger or irritation, but your cat's tail can also be used to communicate signs of friendship and pleasure.

The natural tail position for a walking cat lies at half mast, trailing out prettily behind the cat, just above the ground. But when a cat sees a family member or a person that he likes, he will raise his tail vertically like a flag pole as a clear sign of friendly greeting.

Teaching a cat to come when called can be fun.

It isn't just about friendliness though.

The cat tail up signal is also a sign of respect and is offered more frequently from socially 'low-ranking' cats to individuals that are considered important or superior. Just like a handshake, the tail up signals that the cat's intentions are friendly and unaggressive. And in studies the tail up signal has been shown to reduce aggression in other cats, so it acts as a defence mechanism and fight avoidance tool. That makes it a pretty neat signalling device!

Back arching and rolling in happy cats

The iconic cat winding himself around his owner's legs, with an arched back and high tail, is a well-known sight often represented in art and photography. Most cats only offer this behaviour to people they know well. This arched body shape is not fully understood, but it is often associated with cats that are soliciting food. It's different from the arched back of a frightened or angry cat, not only because of the context in which it occurs but because other signs of aggression (which we'll look at below) are absent.

The exaggerated back arch you see in a friendly cat is only possible because the cat's spine is so much more flexible than ours, something that is achieved with the help of some extra vertebrae or backbones. Both Billy and Oscar arch their back like this when they are reminding us that it's mealtime and while we are preparing their food. Most humans find this posture and behaviour very appealing and reinforce it by rewarding the cat.

Rolling is less likely to be associated with food but it is, however, an important signal. A cat that rolls on his back in your presence is giving you a clear message. He is saying, 'I trust you.' Exposing the vulnerable belly area is a big risk for any animal to take and they only do this when they feel safe. If your cat likes to sleep near you in this position it is a sign of friendship. Exposing the belly more briefly during play or greeting is common in young cats and kittens, and is often misinterpreted by humans as an invitation to touch. It usually isn't! When he has just been fed and is relaxed, Billy will often respond to a familiar human voice by rolling on his back and looking up adoringly at them. The temptation to stroke his beautiful fluffy ginger tummy is enormous. It is, however, an amusing trick on his part – if you give in to the temptation to touch (something some members of the family seem to be incapable of resisting) it results in a swipe from a front paw!

Cats usually roll when they are feeling relaxed and playful.

How cats communicate displeasure

While most of us can tell that our cat is annoyed when his tail is lashing, there are more subtle indications of negative feelings that owners may miss. At times it can be difficult to spot signs that a cat is unhappy, especially when it's to do with another feline member of the family. Like most animals, cats avoid a physical fight when possible, and as a first course of action most cats that aren't getting along will simply avoid each other. If cats that don't know or like one another are forced into close proximity, either through densely populated territories or being confined to the same home, the situation may escalate, and communication through sounds and body language will take place

Cats have a range of whole body signals that are responses to feeling threatened. Culminating in the classic 'alarmed cat' with hair standing on end, arched back, flattened ears and a giant puffed up tail. The idea is to make the cat look threatening, a force to be reckoned with. And a big part of this alarm posture is the way that the cat's fur stands up all over his body. To make themselves even more 'scary and big', an alarmed cat will also turn its body sideways to the threat. Obviously, your aim should be to do your best to ensure that your kitten or cat never reaches this point as it shows that the cat is very upset. And most cats will display a range of body postures leading up to, and long before they get to, this state.

The sounds of aggression

Cats are capable of emitting some quite eerie sounds when they are scared or angry, from low ghostly moans, to loud angry shrieks. One of the most distinctive noises made by a seriously angry cat is the spit. It can be quite shocking when you hear a cat spit for the first time. It sounds a bit like a small explosion, or the noise made when you drop water into hot fat. Many single-cat households will never hear this sound, especially if their cat is confined to the home. It's most commonly heard during a conflict between two cats, and is often preceded by hissing, flattened ears and a lowered body posture. Hissing, swatting and posturing using body language can be used to tell another cat they aren't welcome. This can move on to blocking resources such as food and sleeping places, and in the worst instances biting and scratching can also be included. We look at reducing conflict in multi-cat households in more detail in Chapter 16: Cats Behaving Badly

Cats and people – talking and listening

Apart from during conflicts and sexual interactions, most wildcats don't vocalise very much. Cats that live with humans on the other hand may vocalise quite a bit, and some breeds of pedigree cat are extremely vocal.

Spending time with your cat is a great way to build a bond.

With the exception of a mother cat with kittens, communicating with miaows is probably an unnatural behaviour for most adult cats. Feral cats for example are less likely than domestic cats to miaow to one another. Studies show that we humans have a particular preference for the vocalisations made by our companion animals. Humans enjoy chatting and it's likely that individual cats have learned to communicate with humans that way too, despite not naturally using this tool amongst their own species.

Many cats will mew when they want something that a human can provide. Whether it's a meal or access to outdoors, it is a popular attention-seeking device. Some cats learn this more quickly and more thoroughly than others. Some cat breeds and some individual

Playing helps to build bonds and toys on a string help to protect fingers.

cats are much more talkative than others. Oscar is very vocal, whereas Billy rarely makes any noise at all. On Lucy's advice, Pippa had a deliberate policy of ensuring that she did not reinforce Billy's mews as a kitten in order to avoid 'early waking' problems – this may have paid off, or she may just have been lucky! Oscar, on the other hand, has decided that shouting loudly is a great idea and now even uses his voice to call for Alfie, the cat next door!

Understanding how your cat feels by interpreting the signals and sounds that he uses to communicate with you and with other pets can be an immense help when you are settling a new cat into your home, and will help strengthen and deepen the bond between you and your cat. It is very rewarding to see a previously shy rescue cat offering you a raised tail of friendship, and helpful to know that an expanse of tummy fur isn't necessarily an invitation to touch. Knowing how your cat feels will enable you to respect his boundaries, and help him learn to trust you. Ultimately we all want our cat to feel safe and relaxed in our company, a sign of true friendship.

You'll notice that we haven't talked about purring in this chapter. And there is perhaps no greater sign of friendship than a cat snuggled up to his human companion, purring contentedly. Cats do use purring to communicate with their humans and express contentment, but that is just the beginning. In the next chapter we'll find out how purring is inextricably linked with your cat's athletic prowess as a climber.

15

Your Agile Cat

We only have to look at a cat's feet to see that cats are animals adapted for climbing. Their paws are extremely sensitive to pressure and each toe ends in a razor-sharp curved claw that is both retractable and strong, perfect for gripping into tree bark. Despite their reputed nine lives and physical prowess, the domestic cat is by no means invulnerable and falls do sometimes occur – however, survival rates in cats that have fallen from great heights are surprisingly high, and one factor that has been implicated in their recovery is the ability to purr. In this chapter, we'll look at how cats climb, how they land on their feet, and we'll be exploring the connection between life as a climber and purring. Let's first look at the legendary ability of cats to right themselves in mid-air.

The righting reflex

Skill at climbing, like most athletic endeavours, requires practice, and young cats do fall quite frequently to begin with. An ability to fall safely is a significant benefit for an animal that likes to wander about on rooftops, and one skill usually attributed to the cat is that of always landing on his feet. Of course not all legends are true, but the extraordinary ability of the domestic cat to rotate its body in mid-air is no myth.

The righting reflex is the ability of the cat to turn, as he falls, and land the right way up, so that he meets the ground with his paws. Every cat has an area in the brain devoted to this skill, and it isn't something that needs practice. The righting reflex is totally independent of the ability to see. Cats can right themselves during freefall in total darkness and blind cats have just the same righting ability as cats that can see. A cat uses the same organs for balance as we do, the vestibular system buried deep within the inner ears, helped along by the skin and muscles of the torso and neck, but their reflexes are far more sophisticated.

Slow motion video enables us to see exactly how cats right themselves. They always follow the same pattern of movements when they begin to fall. First of all the cat's head moves into the correct position, then the shoulders and mid-section and finally the hindquarters. The whole manoeuvre would not be possible without the flexibility of the cat's elongated spine. The sequence of movements can be repeated if the cat isn't lined up correctly, provided there is time before they hit the ground. It's estimated that the minimum distance from the ground required for the righting reflex to work is around 30 centimetres (12 inches).

High rise syndrome

Of course, not every fall ends safely. Being an adventurous cat is risky. Vets see so many cats who have been involved in falls from great heights that they have a name for the type of injuries that these cats typically sustain: high rise syndrome. Cats presenting in the vet's surgery with high rise syndrome are typically young and active. Playfulness and inexperience in moving around at heights are probably contributory factors. And these kinds of falls are more common in summer months when people are likely to leave upstairs windows open.

One of the features of high rise syndrome in cats is the surprisingly high proportion of survivors. The survival rate among 84 cats in a 2012 study was an astonishing 98.8 per cent (94 per cent if you take into account that a few cats were later euthanised due to their injuries). This is despite

Tail position and sensitive paws help this cat balance on a narrow ledge.

an average height fallen of more than two-and-a-half storeys. One explanation for this survival rate may be the cat's ability to purr, and science can offer an explanation as to why that may be.

How cats purr

Most cat lovers like to hear their cat purring. And we have seen that it can also be used as a form of communication. True purring is an unusual behaviour in the animal world as a whole. It only occurs in the cat family, and the closely related civets and genets. When scientists talk about true purring they are describing a sound that is created in quite a different way from the noises we and most other animals make.

We have a larynx, or voice box, in our throats just as cats and other mammals do. But when we speak or sing or when our dogs bark or when a horse neighs, that sound is created and moderated by the flow of air over our vocal chords inside the voice box. In order to speak, sing or hum, most animals need to breath out. That flow of air through our vocal chords is controlled just as we control our breathing, but in a more conscious way, using our diaphragms and the muscles in our chest.

It isn't possible for us to generate sounds without breathing, but cats have the ability to do just that. You'll probably have noticed that cats can purr when they are eating, and they purr when breathing in as well as when breathing out. That's because cats can vibrate their vocal chords without forcing air over them. It's this unique and clever skill that creates the wonderful sounds in your cat's throat. It's even possible for a cat to purr while vocalising in other ways.

The purpose of purring

We tend to think of purring as a sign of contentment. Many cats purr when they are being stroked, when greeting family members and when kneading themselves off to sleep. Cats also use purring to communicate their needs or wants to their human families. Scientists call this behaviour 'solicitation purring'. This distinctive type of purring used at mealtimes, for example, has a ring of urgency about it that even people who don't live with cats are able to recognise.

But cats also sometimes purr when they are stressed or upset-during examinations at the vet's surgery, for example. So you can't rely on purring as a sign that your cat feels happy about the situation he is in. In fact, cats have been known to purr when badly hurt or very frightened. This gives us a clue as to purring's other, more serious side.

We had heard rumours that cats use purring to heal themselves, and even that purring could have healing effects on those in close proximity to a cat, but neither of us were sure if these claims were true or if the healing power of purring was a myth. The evidence we gathered was fascinating, and it is all to do with sound waves and their effects on bones.

How purring may help mend bones

Sound waves vary in frequency depending on how high or low the sound is. Scientists use a unit of measurement called a hertz (Hz) to identify different frequencies. Domestic cats for example purr at a frequency of around 26Hz. In the last few decades quite a lot of research has shown that certain sound waves can have an effect on the body in a range of different ways. One effect that is particularly interesting is the ability of sound waves to influence the rates at which tissues within our body heal after they are injured. Over 20 years ago sounds too high for humans to hear were demonstrated to significantly improve the rate of healing in leg bone fractures in rats. And today, the use of ultrasound is widespread in sports injury clinics, not just for healing bones, but for healing soft tissue injuries too.

Sound waves, even those we cannot hear, make the tissues in our bodies vibrate. And experiments have shown that it is the mechanical vibration itself that has the extraordinary effect of helping broken bones to mend.

Domestic cats purr at a much lower audible pitch of around 26Hz, or 26 cycles per second. A study on rabbits comparing a range of different frequencies discovered that the sound frequency with the most powerful healing effect was around 25Hz. It looks like the mythical power of purring is not a myth after all, our cats have evolved their very own healing mechanism. And this ability to purr themselves better may in part account for the high recovery rate in cats that are injured in falls.

So your amazing cat has both an ability to fall safely and would appear to possess the ability to accelerate his own healing process if he does fall and injure himself. But what about cats that don't fall? What about cats that simply get … stuck?

Coming down takes more practice than going up.

Why do cats get stuck in trees?

We have all heard of firefighters running ladders up trees to rescue trapped cats, and have watched cats being rescued on TV. But if cats are such great climbers, so well adapted to life in the tree-tops, how come so many of them get stuck in trees?

It's all to do with your cat's anatomy. Their claws are designed to very effectively latch into a surface and pull themselves up or along. Retractable curved talons hook onto the tree trunk while strong back legs push their weight upwards. But in the opposite direction, the mechanics don't work so well. The curved claws no longer provide a grip and the front end of the cat isn't strong enough to provide support. On trees with low branches a cat will simply jump to the ground, but on trees with a long straight trunk a cat needs to go down backwards, and that is simply not a natural direction for a cat to want to face.

Fortunately, providing an unpleasant experience as a youngster doesn't put them off altogether, climbing down backwards is a skill that older cats seem to acquire with practice.

Your predatory friend

Your cat's climbing ability has an underlying purpose, which is to enable him to be a more efficient and successful predator. Powerful hunting instincts are an important part of what makes a cat a cat, but they can also bring cats into conflict with their human housemates. In Part 3 we look at how to solve some common behaviour problems in cats. We'll also cover a range of other challenges that life with a feline companion will inevitably throw at you, from hairballs to health troubles to old age.

Playing with toys helps your cat practise and refine his hunting skills.

3

Problem
Solving

16

Cats Behaving Badly

Falling out of love with our cat is not something that any of us plan when we bring home a kitten, but when a loved one behaves badly on a regular basis it is natural for our tolerance and patience to wear thin. Sometimes behavioural problems start gradually and creep up on us, others sweep in with plenty of drama. Either way, pets that soil in the house, pets that are destructive or aggressive, or who prevent their families sleeping, can be a huge challenge.

Undesirable behaviour can result in companion animals being relinquished to animal shelters or even euthanised, so resolving behaviour problems quickly, and better still preventing them happening in the first place, is the key to ensuring that cats remain loved and valued members of their family.

That's what this chapter is all about. We'll be talking about the most common problems that people experience with their cats, such as spraying, scratching, biting and boredom, and looking at ways to treat them when they occur, or better still avoid them altogether.

Early waking

Cats, of course, do not consider early waking to be a problem. If allowed access to human sleeping areas, many cats consider it their duty to ensure that two-legged occupants of the house are up and about making breakfast before the sun is over the horizon.

When Oscar was a kitten he had free run of the house throughout the day and night. For a while that worked really well. Family members loved having him snuggled up on the end of the bed – he was great company, and if he wanted to leave the room he did so quietly and without disturbing the peace. Sadly, this didn't last.

Oscar likes to chat to anyone who will listen.

By the time he had grown up a little, Oscar found his voice. Some cats, like the gorgeous Siamese, are renowned for being chatty. Oscar is just a normal black and white moggy, but to hear him exercise his vocal chords gives you cause to contemplate his ancestry. During the day this isn't an issue. He's a friendly boy and will greet people with a purr and miaow, or ask for his dinner at regular intervals. But at some point in those early months, Oscar decided that 11pm and 3am were important times for the family to get together for a bit of a snack. Unsurprisingly, this wasn't very well received. After all, Oscar had access to the cat flap to go outside if he needed to relieve himself and, let's face it, it wasn't exactly a mealtime.

If your cat decides to rouse the family just as they are drifting off to sleep, or at some unseemly hour before dawn, you may need to rethink their privileges. Lucy managed to restore peace to the bedrooms by shutting Oscar downstairs when she retired to bed. In an open plan house this could be more tricky but simply shutting your bedroom door so that the cat cannot join you is usually effective. It may take a few nights before the cat gives up miaowing outside your room and scratching at the door, but if you don't respond to him at all, he will eventually abandon hope of persuading you to join him. Ignoring his cries might be hard, but it is the key to a quiet night in the long run. In the meantime, grab some headphones and listen to some music or an audiobook to help reduce *your* urges to behave in an equally unreasonable fashion.

Most cats don't consider early waking to be a problem.

The trouble with spraying

Cats have the interesting ability to pee backwards. The purpose of this is to leave a powerful scent mark on an item that the wish to identify as associated with them. You may have heard that tomcats may spray inside their homes if they are not neutered. But you might be surprised to hear that up to 10 per cent of all cats spray in adulthood. That's right, it's not just male cats who spray! While the problem is more common in entire males, it does occur in female cats and in neutered males too. Marking in neutered cats is more common where cats are coming into conflict with other cats, both inside and outside the home.

There are things you can do at home to help the situation. While spraying isn't usually about answering the call of nature, improving litter box hygiene can make a difference and for some cats can resolve the issue completely. An increased hygiene routine is a good first step to try.

If the spraying has started spontaneously, it's time to take your cat to the vet. There are some medical treatments available for the issue and your vet is the best person to assess your cat's needs and give him what they believe to be the most appropriate drug.

Destructive scratching

Cats scratch their claws over your furniture and fittings for a range of reasons. The act of scratching stretches the tendons and muscles in the toes and may help to keep them supple. Scratching helps to remove the dead outer casing from claws exposing the nice sharp new interior and keeping the claws in tip top condition for climbing. Scratching can also be a form of territorial marking and free roaming cats have been shown to focus on scratching points on routes around the perimeter of their home range.

Cats prefer a fairly rough surface for scratching purposes. Outdoors, they often use wood – fence posts, gates and tree trunks are popular. Indoors, cats like to scratch on coarse carpet, traditional basketwork or rattan, and the fabric covers of upholstered furniture. With their razor-sharp claws even a kitten has the potential to do a lot of unsightly damage if allowed unsupervised access to valuable furniture.

We'll look at solutions to scratching indoors in a moment, but there is one solution that we don't recommend. And that is declawing. This is a surgical procedure involving the amputation of the ends of the toes of a cat. In Australia, New Zealand, much of Western Europe and in some cities in the

Cats prefer rough wood like this old gate for scratching.

USA declawing is banned. Even if you live in a region where declawing is still an option we strongly recommend that you do not choose to have your cat's toes amputated. It is definitely not in your cat's best interests and, fortunately, there are ways to deal with these concerns which don't involve such drastic measures.

Preventing destructive scratching

The way to avoid your cat disassembling the arms of your favourite chair or digging up the carpet on your stairway is to provide more attractive scratching points throughout your home.

Cats like to scratch on an upright surface that is at least a metre high. That means they can stretch their whole body out as they reach upwards and grip onto the surface. Cats prefer rope or carpet-covered surfaces to card, and many manufactured scratching posts are covered in rope or string. They also prefer a narrow pole to one with a broad base. In other words, you are simulating the presence of a tree trunk in your home.

Make sure that you have enough scratchers – if your cat can't find one easily, he'll be much more tempted to use the couch. Admittedly scratchers are not the prettiest items, and finding ones to complement your decor may be challenging. However, inappropriate scratching decreases with age and is more likely to be a problem in kittens and younger cats, so it's possible that you will be able to reduce the number of cat scratching posts that you provide in your home over time. And if one day your cat is allowed outdoors, you may be able to remove them altogether.

Deliberate scratching is not the only way that cats can damage furniture. Many house cats are good at keeping their claws withdrawn, walking across the furniture using the soft pads of their paws. But, there is no guarantee that those claws won't come out from time to time and leave tiny pin pricks in your furniture. Especially where a cat needs them in order to balance. Pippa has some tiny marks in her leather sofa from Billy's claws when he was a kitten, for example. To begin with, it might be sensible to leave your favourite antique leather chair in a room that the cat does not have access too.

My cat is biting and scratching me!

Few behavioural situations are as sad for an owner as aggression. With kittens, rough use of teeth and claws is usually a passing phase. When Oscar was a kitten he would wrap his own legs around the arm or leg of his antagonist and then sink his teeth in. This is pretty typical kitten play and often directed at family members that tease! Less teasing and the use of toys that don't involve hands is the way to go.

In an older cat, however, aggression can be trickier to manage. The following steps will help.

Step 1: Health check

If a previously unaggressive cat starts to bite out of the blue, then a trip to the vet is in order to make sure that there isn't a medical reason that your pet is feeling tetchy. Cats, like so many creatures, are great at masking pain. When they are ill, seemingly unrelated behavioural changes like this may be early clues that something might be wrong.

If your cat is in good health, then the next step is to look for another underlying cause of aggression. And the likely culprits are fear or stress.

Step 2: Reducing fear

It's natural for cats to be fearful of the unknown. Socialisation as kittens is the process that enables cats to live comfortably among human beings. Adult cats who are fearful or nervous are more likely to be aggressive than cats who are confident and at ease in their surroundings.

If you have adopted a feral or semi-feral cat, or one who has been nervous throughout their lives, then you will need to respect his personal boundaries and minimise handling in order to build a bond between you.

Reducing fear means anticipating situations that your cat won't like, such as being picked up or the sight of a visitor's dog in the kitchen, and avoiding them where possible. It's important not to expect too much of a nervous cat, and more a question of 'managing' the situation than attempting to turn your timid friend into a cuddly lap cat.

One technique that can help fearful cats is a process called counter-conditioning. This is where you associate something the cat really likes (usually food) with the situation that scares them. This is normally carried out in stages with the fearful pet gradually becoming accustomed to closer and closer approximations of the source of their fear. It's often a process best supervised by a professional behaviourist and your vet should be able to recommend one to you.

Step 3: Reducing stress

There is an overlap between fear and stress, but it will be obvious when your cat is afraid whereas stress may go unnoticed. Reducing environmental stressors, or things that cats find upsetting in and around your home, will go a long way to help a cat that is biting or scratching people. We've seen repeatedly through this book that cats don't like change. New places, new people and especially new cats can be stressful, and the most well-balanced cat may react to stress by displaying aggressive behaviour.

If you have multiple cats make sure each has their own space. If you have just bought a puppy or a new baby home, make sure that the cat can escape to their own space whenever they want to.

Try not to heap stressors upon stressors. If you have just moved home, this isn't a good time to change your cat's brand of food or introduce a new style of litter box.

Attention seeking

While ill health, stress and fear are often the root cause of biting, they are not the only culprits. Sometimes healthy and confident cats will bite, and it is an attention-seeking behaviour. Billy will do this occasionally if he is repeatedly soliciting food and being ignored. This kind of bite is not usually hard, but nor is it acceptable. The best way to deal with it is to remove yourself from the cat, and make sure that he doesn't receive any kind of reward for his rudeness.

Cats that regularly bite for attention are often bored. And finding ways to enrich your cat's environment is a great way to improve his behaviour.

Entertaining your cat

Cats are hardwired to hunt and given access to the opportunities, most of them will spend time doing so each and every day. Kept indoors, cats can easily become bored and irritable. If it has been raining heavily for several days, Pippa will often find Billy amusing himself by tipping over photo frames and pulling hearth rugs around. When the weather is good, he gets rid of his excess energy outdoors and is a more contented and relaxing companion when he comes home.

While it can be challenging to keep a fit young cat entertained in the home, it's worth making the effort in order to have a contented and trouble free feline house-mate. Some of the ways in which you can enrich your cat's environment are cheap or even free. Others are more costly. Together they include:

- Food puzzle toys
- Scratching posts
- Perches and cat trees
- Boxes and tunnels
- Activity wheels
- Outdoor enclosures.

Even the nicest cats get themselves into trouble occasionally.

Eating is a source of great pleasure for cats, yet all too often a pet's meal provides them with nothing but nutrition. You can turn your cat's dinner into a much more stimulating experience by breaking mealtimes into lots of small feeds rather than one giant feast. You can hide food inside cardboard boxes among scrunched-up balls of paper, or in toys designed to dispense one or two pieces of food each time a cat interacts with them. Most cats love exploring dark spaces. Try placing food inside cat tunnels, or make your own hidey holes and tunnels using cardboard boxes taped together.

Some cats enjoy puzzle boxes filled with small toys. Multiple scratching posts around the home are a source of interest to most cats. And cat trees and perches provide cats with the opportunity to climb, balance and observe the world from above. Encouraging a cat to chase a few feathers or a toy on the end of a piece of string helps to satisfy hunting urges and provides a little exercise too.

A significant addition to the indoor cat owner's potential anti-boredom arsenal in recent years has been the arrival of the cat exercise wheel. At around four feet in diameter, and with a significant price tag, this is not a piece of kit that many small homes can accommodate, but if you have the funds and space it is worth considering.

Catnip and cats

You can't live with cats for long without being made aware of the existence of catnip, as many cat toys for purchase have catnip added to them. Catnip is a herb that puts some cats into an excited or aroused state. In other words, it gets them 'high'. Not unreasonably, some new cat owners worry that buying catnip toys for a cat could be considered the equivalent of smearing your toddler's rattles in cannabis resin. Indeed, a study published in the 1960s on the effects of catnip on humans noted that patients reported a very similar effect.

Let's take a closer look at catnip before we pass a verdict on this interesting plant. Catnip contains a naturally occurring chemical called nepetalactone. It is in no way unique in the effect it produces on cats – in fact there are 14 chemical compounds altogether that can produce the behaviour changes we see in cats that are affected by catnip. Not all cats are susceptible to the charms of this little herb, but for those that are (including both Oscar and Billy) it can provide entertainment for a bored cat in bad weather and help prolong the joys of kittenhood.

Billy loves his catnip mice.

Catnip doesn't seem to have any untoward side effects, and may even help cheer up a cat that is going through a bad patch. In 2017 Oscar was quite badly injured in a fight with another cat. He was healing well and under veterinary care, but the poor boy totally lost his sparkle. A kind colleague who had stumbled upon Lucy's crochet website suggested that a crochet catnip mouse would be well received. And how right they were! The quickly put-together toy flicked a switch. Oscar went from a lethargic furry ball who wouldn't stop trying to remove his cone to the fired up killing machine we all know and love in 30 seconds flat.

17
Horrible Hairballs and Other Furry Facts

Cats are hairy. There is no denying it. Even the short-haired varieties carry a vast amount of fluff wherever they go, and leave generous traces of it wherever they have rubbed their faces or laid their bodies for a rest.

Grooming a long-haired cat with the right tools can help reduce the amount of fur that's strewn across your furniture. But it's a job that can be challenging unless you go about it in the right way! In this chapter we'll look at how you can teach your cat to accept being groomed, and at what you'll need to do to keep his beautiful fur coat in tip top condition. We'll also look at the role that self and social grooming plays in a cat's life and at how to cope with the unpleasant problem of hairballs.

Your cat probably won't appreciate your attempts to smarten him up, nor recognise the need for you to do so. After all, he already spends a large part of his day keeping himself in order. Great attention to detail when washing is part of the feline personality and every cat is aided and abetted by a very useful tool – a special kind of tongue.

How cats keep themselves clean

Cats' tongues are fascinating things. Unlike the soft wet lick from a dog, a lick from a cat's tongue feels scratchy and abrasive. That's because a cat's tongue is covered in tiny barbs that point backwards towards the throat. Called filiform papillae, these little barbs are shorter at the front of the tongue and become larger and sharper in the centre. A spiked tongue serves several useful purposes, from picking up water and scraping meat from bones to grooming. The barbs act like a comb, removing dirt and dust from your cat's coat and helping to prevent matting. Cats spend up to 10 per cent of their waking hours grooming themselves. And it isn't only their own fur that cats like to keep clean and tidy.

A cat's tongue feels rough because it is covered with tiny barbs.

Social grooming in cats

At times, cats that live alongside other cats may spend time grooming one another. This social form of grooming is known as allogrooming. It seems to be a way to reinforce bonds between individuals in the group. Cats are more likely to groom each other when they are familiar with each other, but this is also strongly linked to whether or not they are related. Kittens from the same litter, for example, will be more likely to groom each other than those from different family groups.

Allogrooming is often focused specifically on the head and neck area. The cat who is doing the grooming is more likely to be a higher-ranking individual and will normally position themselves physically higher up than the groomed cat. At first glance allogrooming appears to be a very friendly activity. However, studies show that around a third of grooming sessions is accompanied by some degree of aggression. This usually occurs at the end of the grooming session and is initiated by the dominant cat or groomer. Experts have concluded that social grooming in cats may have evolved as a way to diffuse the tension caused by having to live in close contact with other cats.

Whether or not your cat is grooming themselves or another cat, licking fur inevitably results in swallowing a certain amount of it. And that, as you probably know, can be a problem for cats and for their families. Because what goes down, often comes back up again ...

Horrible hairballs!

It may seem a strange topic for research, but scientists have figured out that as much as two-thirds of the hair your cat loses every year ends up in their poop. In some cats this seems to pass straight through the digestive system, and in others it makes a regular unwelcome return. Hairballs are caused by an accumulation of hair that is swallowed during the course of self-grooming by your cat. The strands of hair that the cat swallows tend to get tangled up with the mucus or slime that protects the lining of your cat's stomach. In a short-haired healthy cat, this doesn't usually cause a problem and if the hairballs build up your cat will just bring them up, hopefully outside in the garden, but sometimes on your carpet. Not very nice, but not very dangerous. However, there is a risk that a large hairball can cause an obstruction in your cat's intestine. And this can be a potentially life-threatening medical emergency.

Having a cat that suffers from hairballs on a regular basis is no joke. If you've ever lived with a cat that suffers from them, you'll know the sound of the tell-tale cough that heralds an episode of vomiting. Hairballs are not exactly balls, in fact they are usually poop shaped – if you come across a regurgitated hairball you could be forgiven for thinking that your cat had pooped in the middle of your carpet. On closer inspection you'll find that a hairball consists of lumps of hair mixed with partly digested food.

Many cats vomit up hairballs with monotonous regularity, while other cats rarely or never do so. Hairballs are not just an unpleasant fact of life for many cat parents, in some cases they can also cause a serious obstruction. It's important that all cat owners are aware of how to recognise this at an early stage. Signs include sudden unexplained loss of appetite, which should never be ignored in a cat. Vomiting and dramatic weight loss are also possibilities. Hairballs are also thought to cause the cat abdominal pain. If you are unsure whether your cat is showing these signs it's always best to check with your vet without delay.

Interestingly, hairball problems are more likely to occur if the cat hasn't eaten for a prolonged period of time. This is thought to be because the food helps to propel the hairball along the digestive tract. So a strategy that might help is to break your cats daily food ration into more frequent, smaller meals.

Cats spend up to 10 per cent of their waking hours grooming themselves.

Special food for hairball sufferers

If your cat suffers from frequent hairballs, one of the options that may be presented to you is to switch to a hairball-reducing cat food. But do they really help, or is it just a marketing ploy?

There is some evidence that a high level of sugar cane fibre in cat food can reduce hairballs in cats by helping them along the gut and out the other end! A study published in 2015 found that increasing levels of dietary fibre in long-haired cats' food caused them to pass more fur through their system and out the other end. However, this effect was not replicated in the short-haired cats in the study. This suggests that if you are a long-haired cat owner a high-fibre hairball cat food is worth giving a go, but if your cat's coat is on the short side, it may not have an impact.

Another way to help reduce the hairball problem is to groom your cat regularly yourself.

Grooming your cat

Grooming isn't a complete cure for hairballs, but it definitely helps. It reduces the volume of loose hair in your cat's fur and therefore reduces the amount of hair that is available for your cat to swallow. Grooming a cat isn't always as simple as it sounds because, unlike dogs, many cats dislike being handled, especially on certain parts of their body. However, there are ways around this problem. It's all about routines and providing an incentive for your cat. For a short-haired cat you'll need a bristle brush.

Billy being groomed after playing in the fireplace.

If your cat has never been groomed before, the first step is simply to persuade your cat to see the brush itself as something great. So place the brush on the table where you intend to groom your cat and have a pot of tasty treats ready. Pick the brush up, give the cat a treat, and put the brush down again. Repeat several times, then start to give the cat a few gentle sweeps with the brush before each treat, starting at the head and working backwards. Keep each session very short to begin with.

With long-haired cats, you'll need to use a metal comb or rake. If your cat doesn't like being picked up at all, start by dealing with this problem first. There are step by step instructions in Chapter 13: Training and Tricks. If you only groom your cat once in a blue moon, or after a hairball vomiting event, your cat is probably going to head for high ground as soon as he sees the brush appear. Instead, dedicate a few minutes each day to grooming, so that he becomes accustomed to it. When it comes to incentives, all cats are motivated by food if they are hungry enough.

It's worth reiterating that you need to subtract the food you use in training, from your cat's daily food allowance in order to avoid your cat adding to his problems with an ever-expanding waistline. You'll also want to train when your cat is most likely to be hungry so have your grooming sessions just before his mealtime.

Caring for whiskers

People sometimes ask us if it's okay to cut their cat's whiskers. The answer is definitely NO. Interestingly, sometimes, mother cats will 'trim' their kittens' whiskers. Scientists have hypothesised that the mother cat may be trying to keep kittens close to the nest. However, that doesn't mean you can dive for the scissors and join in. We discussed the role of whiskers in Chapter 1, and they're an important sensory organ for your cat. Being deprived of whiskers could well be stressful and disorientating. It is neither necessary nor beneficial to cut them.

Sometimes a cat's whiskers are removed accidentally by an over enthusiastic groomer. If that has happened to your cat don't panic – they will grow back eventually, but it could take a couple of months or so before your cat is returned to his former glory!

Do cats need baths?

Cats are notorious for their cleanliness, but also for their distaste for entering the water. Unlike their messy canine cousins, it's very rare for most cats to ever need a bath. Billy has never had a bath. At six years old Oscar has only had one, after he managed to jump into an open pot of emulsion – a moment that was comedic in hindsight, but quite stressful and scratchy at the time. Fortunately, he was only a few months old when the incident occurred, and so fitted nicely and fairly simply into the kitchen sink along with some lukewarm water and an old tea towel.

Bathing your cat is generally not necessary unless they have managed to get themselves covered in something sticky, smelly or toxic. If you do find your cat is in need of a bath, keep it simple. You'll need a small tub with lukewarm water, some cat-safe shampoo and a couple of old towels. And preferably a friend to help. Make sure the water level doesn't come above his knees, and gently pop your cat in. He will probably be unimpressed with the experience, so you might need that friend handy to gently hold on to him. Lift a little water over the areas that need attention, rub in some shampoo, then work it into a lather. Gently rinse and wrap your cat up in a clean, dry, towel. Make sure you don't get your cat's face wet unless you really have to, and avoid shampoo going anywhere near his eyes, nose or mouth.

Coping with cat hair in the home

Most people have an idea of how they want their home to look, and a light to moderate sprinkling of cat hair is not usually involved. If you are extremely keen on keeping your rooms in a show-home condition, then throwing a pet into the mix can be stressful. But there are ways to maintain a fairly nice environment even with the fluffiest of cats. It does involve having the right tools for the job, and a keen eye for the strange places that fur can end up.

An essential piece of kit for the fur-averse cat owner is a good pet hair vacuum cleaner, together with one of the multiple attachments that allow you to suck the fluff from your sofa as well as around the edges of the carpet.

A manual pet hair removal tool is also helpful for those unexpected furry locations. This is a hand-held brush that comes with a separate cleaning box. You simply insert the furry brush into the box and it removes the hair for you. Oscar likes to nestle up against the curtains on the windowsill in Lucy's living room where he can watch the world go by. This leaves a fine coating of hair on the curtains. The vacuum is too powerful and sucks up the fabric, but the pet hair remover is the perfect tool for the job.

We are also great fans of robot vacuums. These clever machines can be scheduled to whiz back and forth over your floor and pick up small amounts of background hair and dirt on a daily basis. They are a brilliant addition to any home with hairy inhabitants, and we like that they force us to keep our floors tidy!

Start as you mean to go on

If you have a long-haired cat, a specialist food and regular grooming may help to reduce the number of hairballs he brings up. But it is still important to keep an eye out for any signs of a gut obstruction and to contact the vet immediately if you are in any doubt.

Cats can be taught to tolerate regular grooming and like so many other aspects of pet care, these procedures are easier for the cat to adapt to if started at an early age. For fast results associate grooming with food and keep sessions short. Ideally by five or six months old your cat will be used to regularly being picked up and will tolerate being brushed or combed by members of the family.

18
Neutering and Sexual Maturity

Most vets advise pet owners to neuter their cats and dogs, and that makes sense on a general population level. Kittens are often able to breed long before they are mentally mature and even before they are fully grown, so unless you take action your small furry friend could soon be adding to the local cat population. However, recent research has complicated matters a little. Only a few years ago neutering pets was seen as an entirely beneficial procedure with not much in the way of unwanted side effects, apart from the small risk inherent in any surgical procedure. But there is now growing awareness that there can be both pros and cons to de-sexing our pets.

In this chapter we'll look at the positives and negatives, and at what's involved in neutering your feline friend, so that you can make the best decision for the welfare of your pet and your family. We'll start by looking at what happens if you don't neuter your cat. Let's talk about sexual maturity and seasons!

Sexual maturity in male cats

Most male cats become sexually mature before their first birthday. Some may become sexually active before they are nine months old. Left entire, male cats develop a noticeably broader face than their sisters. This is due to the development of pads of fat in the cheeks which help to protect the male cat from injury in the event of a fight. A study carried out in Portsmouth dockyards in the 1980s concluded that older males probably develop a dominance hierarchy to avoid or reduce conflict, but for younger males fighting is a fact of life. The reality is that if you do

Tomcats have a wider face than their sisters.

not have your male cat castrated he will incur some level of injury from fighting in his youth. He will also roam over considerable distances in order to find opportunities to mate. This roaming also puts him at increased risk from road traffic accidents.

Male cats are somewhat territorial in that they may prefer to 'stake out' an area, and may even be reluctant to mate in an unfamiliar location. They also like to mark out their territory using body scent. They do this in two ways – by rubbing their cheeks on objects within that territory and by spraying urine on those objects. Spraying is distinctive and separate from urinating for the purposes of emptying the bladder. It's the equivalent of the dog cocking his leg on every lamp-post. When spraying, the male cat will back up against a wall, fence or other vertical surface and has the ability to direct urine backwards. He'll spray as high as he can for maximum distribution of scent. One of the problems of this habit, of course, is that in some sexually mature male cats it isn't restricted to outdoors.

Spraying in the home is a problem that can arise if you decide not to have your cat castrated. One option is to wait and see if your entire male cat starts spraying and then have him castrated if he does. The problem with this option is that castration is not effective at curing this problem in all cases. Neutering much later in life can be problematic in other ways too. Sexual behaviour in neutered male cats with previous sexual experience has been shown to persist for weeks or even months after castration

So, key common problems that are at increased risk of occurring with a male cat that has not been neutered include:

- Injuries from fighting
- Injuries or death from road accidents
- Inappropriate urination in the home.

These are not all inevitable. For example, not all tomcats spray in the home (though many do), and if your entire male cat is never allowed outdoors, only the last of those three will apply. Note also that neutering is not a guarantee that a male cat will never urine mark in the house. A small percentage of castrated males will do so, especially in multiple cat households.

But those three factors are the basic risks you take if you choose not to neuter your boy. And those are the reasons that the majority of us will bite the bullet, albeit with some sadness for what might have been, and take our male kittens to have their boy bits removed.

Sexual maturity in female cats

Female cats have their first season and become pregnant at around six months old, but it can happen even earlier. If you are used to dogs with their twice-yearly seasons, your female cat may take you by surprise. If she is not mated she'll come into season again and again at approximately three-week intervals. And she'll make quite a song and dance about it too.

Female cats in heat become restless and noisy. The purpose of this calling is to attract the attention of male cats, and if the female isn't mated it will persist for several days. Some female cats in season will respond to being touched or stroked by their owners by raising their bottom in the air, but not all do, so lack of this response isn't a guarantee that your cat is not in heat. Once a cat has been mated, and only after mating, she ovulates, and her season will end after a few days whether or not she becomes pregnant. If she isn't mated her season may continue for another week or more.

To prevent a female cat from being mated she must be either neutered or kept permanently and securely indoors. If a sexually mature female is allowed outside the chances are, she will become pregnant. There are intact male cats in virtually every region. Pregnancy can occur during your cat's very first season, even though she is still a kitten herself. Pregnancy lasts for about nine weeks and a female cat can become pregnant again immediately after birth.

You can see that unless you have your female cat neutered by the time she is around six months old, you are going to be responsible for an endless stream of kittens each and every year, and repeated pregnancies are unlikely to be beneficial to your female cat's health.

In a few months' time this kitten will be capable of having kittens of her own.

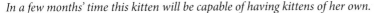

Many kittens are neutered when they are six to eight months old.

The best age to neuter a cat

Traditionally, most vets have recommended that cats are neutered at between six and eight months of age. But there is a growing trend for neutering at an earlier age, especially in animal shelters and cat rescues. An American study on the risks and benefits of early neutering in cats was published in 2004 and found that early neutering reduced the risk of urine spraying, the risk of asthma, aggression towards veterinarians and the risk of gum disease. It also, however, increased the risk of hiding and shyness. This is in keeping with findings in dogs, where neutering in males has been associated with nervousness, presumably because testosterone is a confidence-building hormone. Because of this, and knowing that Billy was going to have to cope with the world outside, with the potential for interaction with the numerous other cats in the village, Pippa decided to wait until Billy was at least six months old before having him castrated. It's likely that your own vet will have a preference, and some may suggest early neutering. But the final decision is yours, and if your kitten is on the nervous side you might want to wait a little while to allow his confidence to grow. In the meantime, as some kittens become sexually active much earlier than the average, keeping an entire kitten indoors is a wise precaution.

Concerns about neutering

We now know that removing sex hormones has the potential to influence far more than reproductive capacity and behaviour. Studies in dogs have shown that neutering can be associated with increased risk of joint problems and a range of different types of cancer, and the release of data from the Swiss Feline Cancer Registry in 2016 highlights a similar issue in cats.

There is also evidence that neutering is associated with obesity. When neutered and unneutered male cats were compared in one study, they saw a considerable increase in the weight gained as fat in the neutered males. Neutered male cats choose to eat more than their intact counterparts. This doesn't mean of course that your cat will necessarily get fat after being neutered, but it is something to be aware of

Every surgical procedure carries some risk too. There's a small possibility of infection and complications from anaesthesia. But neutering is a widely practiced procedure and complication are unusual.

Some people allow their female cat to have at least one litter before neutering her. The reasons for this are probably complex, but one common myth is that it is beneficial to the cat. We couldn't find any evidence at all to support this view.

The operation

Neutering is a fairly simple procedure for a male cat. Under general anaesthetic, a tiny incision is made in the scrotum, the testes are removed and the incision stitched. With a female cat the operation is more involved.

Traditionally spaying in a dog or cat involves making a significant incision in the belly and removing the ovaries and uterus. This is a major surgical procedure and there is a recovery time of a couple of weeks, with a large wound to take care of. There is a potential alternative to this major operation. In recent years the laparoscopic spay has become more popular in dogs and a study published in 2015 reported on tests of this procedure in cats.

Laparoscopic spays involve several much smaller incisions in the belly – just big enough to pass a tube containing a camera and the laparoscopic instruments which the vet manipulates via a video feed. The main difference for the cat is that only the ovaries are removed. There is no hysterectomy (removal of the uterus) and the wounds are much smaller. Simply removing the ovaries has been shown to be an effective form of birth control as it removes the hormones necessary to bring the cat into season and to prepare the uterus for pregnancy.

Pippa has had a dog spayed using this method and would definitely choose a laparoscopic spay over traditional surgery in the future. Recovery time for a laparoscopic spay is less, there may be no cone needed as there is no significant incision for the animal to pull at and studies suggest that there is less pain for the animal too. The downside is expense. Spays are not covered by pet insurance and a laparoscopic spay is usually more expensive. Not all vets have the necessary equipment or skills to carry out the procedure on cats, so at the time of writing you may have to travel further afield to get this done. However, we think it's likely that the procedure will become more mainstream in the future.

Neutering – the bigger picture

In the USA where neutering is widespread, a 2009 study estimated that 80% of cats are neutered. However, a survey of cat owning households in the UK in 2007 found that only 66 per cent of cats aged six to twelve months are neutered. You only have to look in the online pet adverts here in Britain to see how many kittens are on offer. The general consensus in the veterinary literature is that this is a bad thing, and that early neutering is beneficial. The literature also questions why vets in the UK haven't adopted early neutering more widely. That may be more to do with their clients than with the vet's themselves. It's not beyond the realms of possibility that most humans who claim their cat has had an unplanned litter are actually well aware that a litter of kittens would be forthcoming.

People tend to fall into three camps when it comes to breeding:

- Adopt don't shop (no one should breed while there are animals in shelters)
- Leave breeding to breeders
- Anyone should be allowed to breed from their pets.

We looked at the first argument in Chapter 6 (pages 46–48); it's basically an ethical decision that only the individual can make. The problem with the second argument is that it assumes that 'breeders' are the best people to be breeding animals, and in some cases this is simply not true. Most people who describe themselves as a cat 'breeder' only breed pure-bred cats and as we saw again in Chapter 6 (page 49); a number of breeds suffer health issues as a direct result of deliberate breeding for disabilities (shortened stature, flattened faces, etc.) and many pure breeds of cat suffer from inbreeding within a very small gene pool.

Neutering should improve your cat's chances of a long and happy life.

When it comes to the argument that everyone should be allowed to breed from their pet, it is clear that not everyone is capable of or willing to raise kittens responsibly without adding to the animal shelter population. However, the stigma that has been attached to home breeding is simply not justified. And there are many kittens born into ordinary homes every year that grow up to make wonderful pets, like Billy and Oscar.

If you are tempted to breed from your cat, wait until they are mature themselves – essentially that will mean keeping your cat indoors for the first year of their lives. Bear in mind that a male cat takes no part in raising his young. You will never see the fruits of his loins and may well have to deal with the fallout from fights.

The influence you have over a cat once they have passed through that cat flap is negligible and the opportunities for birth control non-existent. While there are some health risks to neutering, they have to be weighed against the disadvantages. We believe that for cats and their owners, the benefits of neutering vastly outweigh the risks – especially for cats that are allowed the freedom to roam. As an independent creature, a sexually entire cat is at much greater risk outdoors that a neutered one, but the final decision and the timing of the operation is up to you. If you decide to have your cat neutered, talk to your vet about that timing and ask them about the latest research and techniques.

Keeping our cats healthy is our number one priority. Neutering for outdoor cats is a sensible part of any cat's welfare plan, and should improve their chances of a long and healthy life.

19
Cat Health Problems

Cats of any age will experience health problems from time to time and it's a good idea to get your cat checked regularly to make sure things are still running smoothly. In this chapter we look at some of the main health issues that can affect our feline friends of all ages and give you an idea of what to look out for and when to get help. We also look at opportunities for avoiding health problems in the future, such as by picking structurally healthy breeds or those that are less predisposed to inherited diseases.

Is my cat overweight?

Like most mammals, cats that are significantly overweight are at risk from a number of different health conditions including diabetes, heart problems, and cancer. While chubby cats are cuddly and may look sweet, the truth is that slim cats live longer, healthier lives. Worryingly, at least one in ten, and in some areas as many as four in ten, cats are now overweight. It's a good idea for all cat owners to take a good look at our cat's silhouette from time to time and think hard about whether their waistline needs reducing. But how can you tell if your cat is overweight rather than naturally big?

In some cats it is obvious that they are too fat – a drooping belly is a big give away – but with others it can be hard to decide. The first step is to look down on your cat from above, when they are standing on the ground. A healthy cat will have some indication of a waist – a narrowing of their body just in front of their hips. This can be difficult to judge in a fluffy cat, but what you don't want to see is an oval shape, where the area in front of the hips is wider than the hips themselves. Next, run your hands firmly along your cats flanks. You should just be able to feel ribs underneath that fur. And you'll be able to feel the waist that may have been hard to see in your fluffy cat. If you can't feel ribs when you press firmly, your cat may be overweight.

Slim cats are more likely to be healthy and long lived.

Most owners are able to assess fairly accurately whether their cat is in a healthy weight range, but some do find it difficult. One study found that owners of overweight or really fluffy cats tend to find it harder to judge their kitties' weight accurately. If you are not sure then do pay a visit to your vet who will be able to weigh your cat and put your mind at rest.

Obesity is more common in cats over three years old, neutered males and cats fed on dry food. However, regardless of cause, the only certain way to get those pounds to drop is to make sure that your cat gets less to eat.

Helping your cat lose weight

Reducing calorie intake is important for chubby kitties, and there is no one right way to do it. Some people find switching to a low-calorie cat food is helpful, but that means getting your cat used to a new type of food. The best option is simply to reduce the quantity of your regular brand.

Start by reducing your cat's food ration by a quarter. You are more likely to have success if you measure portions as it is so easy to misjudge quantities. If your cat is miserably hungry, try feeding more often but in smaller quantities. Frequent small meals are a more natural way of feeding for cats and may help to avoid any hungry pleading.

Don't go crazy and cut rations back too far – sudden weight loss can be harmful to your cat and you are aiming for a regular steady decrease. There's no need to cut all pleasure out of your cat's life. In fact, tiny treats given occasionally could even help to keep your cat from begging at the bowl, while strengthening the bond between you!

It can be challenging to slim down a cat with outdoor access. If you suspect your crafty friend is begging food from a neighbour you could have them wear a collar with DO NOT FEED ME printed on it, like Lucy did with Oscar. Or you could try having a chat with your neighbour and explaining that your vet has recommended you slim down your cat for the sake of his health. If all else fails, you might need to keep the cat indoors for a while. Keeping your cat at a healthy weight can normally be achieved in a few weeks through reducing food quantities.

Teeth and dental care

Too much of a good thing can cause problems in other areas too, and what goes into your cat's tummy has to first pass through his mouth.

Periodontitis, commonly known as gum disease, is one of the most frequent health problems faced by modern cats, and if untreated eventually results in the gradual loss of teeth from the jaw. Cats with overcrowded teeth, including flat-faced cats, are at greater risk. Another condition called feline odontoclastic resorptive lesions (FORL) is a progressive disease affecting a significantly high percentage of adult cats. FORL damages teeth along the gumline and can lead to multiple extractions. Teeth can be broken in accidents too, and dental problems can also arise in adult cats as a result of viruses, infections and problems with immune systems. Dental problems can often be treated by your vet, but are best avoided in the first place where possible.

As we have seen, wet food is widely agreed to be the best option for your cat's general health, but harder foods are better for your cat's teeth. One way around this issue is to give your cat soft meals but provide them with dental chews. Dental chews work by encouraging your cat to chew, while maintaining contact with the surface of the tooth onto their textured surface.

While it isn't a guarantee, an appropriate diet and regular vet checks will help to set your cat up for good oral health during their lifetime.

Tummy troubles

If you've had a cat for several years, you have probably had that early morning sinking feeling – the one when you wandered downstairs in your dressing gown, and noticed an unpleasant odour in the air. Most pets have the occasional upset stomach, just like most humans, and it's nothing to worry about. With small kittens more than one bout of vomiting or diarrhoea in the space of a few hours warrants a phone call to the vet. An adult cat that seems alert and is behaving normally can be starved for 24 hours to let their stomach settle, then fed as normal. You might want to reduce their access to bedrooms or rooms with carpets where possible until the worst is over.

When tummy troubles are more frequent or ongoing, that's when it's time to pop down to see the vet and have a chat. Oscar had a spate of vomiting issues when he was around four years old. A visit to the vet ruled out serious concerns and a bit of trial and error revealed that he wasn't getting on with his food anymore. To this day, you can give a couple of particular popular brands of wet food to Oscar and they will be wolfed down, only to revisit us again 30 seconds later. The issue was solved by switching brands, but it remains a mystery what ingredient of these specific products was causing him to have such a dramatic reaction.

Food allergies are not the only possible cause of vomiting. Parasites and infectious diseases are common causes, and if the problem is persistent the only way to get to the bottom of it is to involve your vet.

Bladder problems

Cats are susceptible to urinary tract infections and obstructions. They can cause a cat to strain in the litter box and pass blood in their urine. A cat with a urinary problem may also pee in inappropriate places.

Obstructions are usually cause by uroliths, tiny stones that can develop in the urinary tract. Some pedigree cat breeds are more susceptible to urolithiasis than other cats.

Feline idiopathic cystitis is something that many cat owners will hear the vet mention at some point in their lives. It simply means bladder inflammation of unknown cause. While we can't always find a cause, we do know that urinary tract disease is more common in very fat cats, neutered males, older cats and in cats fed on dry food. However, it can strike any cat, male or female, at any time.

Not only are bladder problems a painful issue for your cat, obstructions can be life threatening if left untreated, so if you notice your cat straining or becoming distressed in the litter box you need to get a same day appointment with your vet.

Heart problems

Heart problems in cats are sadly quite common, particularly in some pedigree breeds, such as the Maine Coon, Abyssinian, Himalayan, Persian, Ragdoll, Birman, Siamese, Sphynx and even the British Shorthair. But it's not just an issue limited to pedigrees, and the nature of the heart problems varies quite a bit.

Symptoms of heart trouble can range from restlessness to lethargy, fainting or shortness of breath to vomiting and even weakness or pain in the hindquarters. Heart disease isn't something you can diagnose or treat at home and you'll need to seek help from your vet. Many of the symptoms of heart disease are due to a shortage of oxygen, and an affected cat may have a blueish colour to his lips, gums and tongue (cyanosis). In healthy mammals the heart and lungs work together to distribute oxygen around the body, and cats with respiratory problems can also present with similar symptoms.

Breathing problems

When someone mentions asthma in connection with cats, it's natural to assume they are talking about an owner's reaction to pet hair. But asthma is actually quite common in our furry friends too. Feline asthma ranges in severity, just as asthma does in humans. In some cats its impact might be very mild, but it can also be severe with serious coughing fits and difficulty breathing. Symptoms of asthma can include wheezing or noisy breathing as well as the symptoms described under heart troubles. Fortunately, it has several possible treatment options and your vet can help you to manage the condition if your cat develops it.

Sometimes pets will wheeze or show signs of cyanosis that only last for a few minutes or hours and then present at the vet apparently brimming with health. If that happens to your cat, it's a good idea to video any symptoms when they occur. This may help your vet to make a diagnosis.

Other respiratory problems can be caused by infections, and we can reduce the risk of some of these with vaccinations. Aspergillosis is a fungal infection that is often found in some breeds of pedigree cat, but is not limited only to them. Your average moggy can suffer from its effects too and it causes trouble breathing. In its most serious form aspergillosis can be fatal.

Skin problems

Although not common in all breeds, skin problems can arise in some with surprising frequency. Did you know for example that cats can suffer from ringworm? (It isn't actually a worm at all but another type of fungus.) Cats can also have skin problems as a result of food allergies, or simply be more likely to suffer due to their breed. Certain cats with unusual coats, or no coat at all like the Sphynx cat, are more prone to various forms of dermatitis. Persian and Himalayan cats may suffer from some forms with a very high frequency. One skin condition, hereditary primary seborrhoea oleosa, is thought to be seen only in Persians.

Skin problems can also arise as a result of unrelated health conditions, and even parasites like mites. Some cats develop nasty skin lesions in response to a mild flea infestation, for example. It may require some detective work to uncover the source of your cat's itching, so if they are scratching, sore, or their coat is looking patchy or thin, it's a good idea to visit the vet.

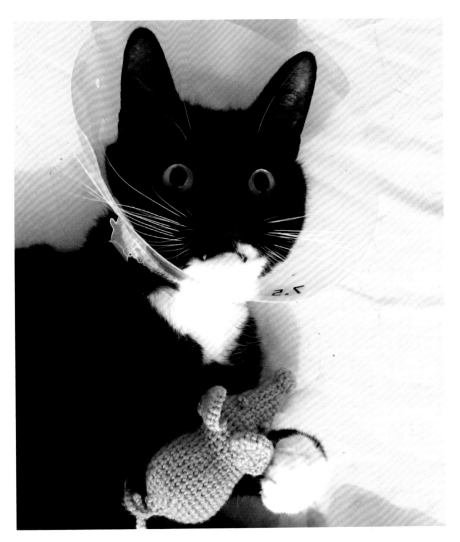

Wearing a cone for a while helped Oscar's bite wound to heal.

Injuries and first aid

Most cats will get the odd scrape or bruise. When a loved pet suffers a significant injury it can be a frightening experience. Fighting with other cats, vehicular close shaves and scrapes on the undergrowth can all result in cuts, bruises, abscesses and even broken teeth or limbs.

Oscar's main adventure was definitely the bite he received from a new cat on the block. The entire surrounding area of tissue became necrotic and he had a massive, horror-movie style open wound on his shoulder for several days. Despite reassurances from the vet that this was perfectly normal, it was still pretty disturbing to see. Fortunately the wound, several centimetres across, healed quickly, and the only medical care Oscar needed was an antibiotic injection, and a plastic cone to stop him chewing at it!

If your cat hurts himself in any way that does not seem to be happy to heal by itself, you obviously need to go and see the vet as soon as you can. Bites and scratches can very easily become infected, and even though cats do heal themselves pretty well they need a helping hand from time to time.

Visiting the vet

Taking the cat to the vet can be a challenge. Cats don't much like car travel or being crammed into a carry crate. However, these proud creatures are extremely good at hiding signs of illness or pain, so when you notice a problem with your cat don't be tempted to ignore it.

If your cat goes off his food, seems lethargic or unusually restless get him checked out. Limping or other signs of pain can be serious. Discharges from eyes, ears or any other part of the body need treating. Panting, wheezing or fainting needs urgent attention, as does any kind of persistent tummy upset. If your cat seems off colour or you are in any doubt that they are not in great health give your vet a call. The vet may be able to reassure you over the phone, but in all probability will want you to bring your cat in for a check-up.

Inherited diseases in cats

While cats in general are a relative healthy and long-lived companion animal, there are a number of inherited diseases that they are susceptible to. Some of these are more common in specific pedigree breeds. They include a number of heart conditions such as hypertrophic cardiomyopathy (HCM) and kidney problems such as polycystic kidney disease (PKD).

Modern DNA tests mean you can now pick a breeder who only breeds from cats that are free from these and other conditions. It's very important when buying a pedigree cat that you not only know which diseases your chosen breed is susceptible to, but also where appropriate ask to see health certificates from the breeder.

Some health conditions are inherited.

Structural problems in cats can also cause health problems, and we've discussed the multiple issues associated with brachycephalic (flat-faced) cats, such as Persians, in some detail in Chapter 5: Different Types of Cat. These problems are inherited too and because they are written into the breed standard they affect every single member of that breed to some extent. This means that the only way to avoid them is to avoid the breed. The other main structural problem to look out for in some cat breeds is dwarfism or shortened legs.

While it's important to acknowledge the genetic problems that are arising in our pure-bred pets, there are some benefits to choosing a pedigree cat. Many of these often very beautiful animals have wonderful temperaments and can make delightful pets. We delve into the world of pedigree cats in Chapter 21 and take a closer look at some examples of popular and unusual pedigree breeds.

The problems of old age

With advances in veterinary care, cats are living longer than ever, and many cats remain fit well into their teens. In the next chapter we'll look at some of the changes you can expect as your cat ages and at how to make the most of those golden retirement years.

20
Your Senior Cat

When you bring home your tiny new kitten, the furthest thing from your mind is where this journey is going to end up. You are far too busy sorting out the practicalities of caring for your new friend and soaking up their cuteness. After a few months, life with a cat becomes normality. You find your own routines. You get used to each other and sometimes barely notice as he snuggles up against you or winds his way around your legs. Life becomes comfortable, and the years slip away.

Time catches up with all of us in the end, but happily old age for cats is often a gentle transition. Most cats slow down a little when they reach their teens but remain physically active throughout their lives. And there are ways that you can help your old friend enjoy his twilight years and, when the time comes, say your peaceful goodbyes in comfort.

Older cats can be very relaxing company.

The good news is that cats are living longer. In the 1990s a study in the USA noted a 100 per cent increase in cats living over seven years compared with the previous decade. There are plenty of benefits to sharing your home with an older cat too. They tend to spend more time around the house and less time bringing home the wildlife. The days of frantic kitten play are long gone. And while kittens are cute, you probably won't miss the crazed clawing at your feet as you try to prepare breakfast or the tripping hazard of a playful ball of fur on your stairs. Older cats move a little less, play a little less and relax a little more.

As a rule of thumb, cats are considered senior from 11 years and geriatric from 15. From a veterinary point of view this simply reflects the increased risk to your cat of certain medical conditions. How *your* cat ages will be influenced by his breed, size, diet, genes, the environment in which he lives and a generous helping of luck.

Although many cats stay fit and healthy for a large proportion of their senior lives, there are bound to be some changes in your cat as the years go by. Some changes are a normal part of ageing, others indicate that something is wrong, and should prompt a visit to the vet.

Normal signs of ageing

Elderly cats vary in appearance with some retaining the glossy coat of their youth for many years, while others look a little moth-eaten as soon as they pass middle age. What many elderly cats do share is a tendency to thinness. In some cases weight loss can indicate health issues, and for that reason it should always be investigated by a vet. If your cat has been passed as healthy, you may be advised to switch to a food specifically designed for elderly cats. We'll talk about that below.

Older cats can also lose some skin elasticity and even have more brittle nails. They may seem a little less energetic and a little less agile than before. Although it may often go unnoticed, elderly cats can also become arthritic and have difficulty moving about. Elderly cats may commonly experience some hearing loss too.

As cats age, their immune systems gradually decline. It's a natural process, and one that is seen in humans and dogs as well. While it may be possible to boost antibody levels in older cats to a certain extent, their immuse system is unlikely to be as efficient as that in younger animals. This means that a senior cat may find it harder to fight off illnesses. Elderly cats may also have less efficient heart and lungs. High blood pressure is a common problem in cats over the age of ten and can damage the eyesight and kidneys.

Declining health is something that we may expect to some extent as we grow older. But just because the natural changes associated with ageing are normal, it doesn't mean we shouldn't seek help from a vet to alleviate them. Studies show that people are more reluctant to get veterinary treatment for cats than for their dogs. That's a shame, because many problems associated with ageing can be successfully treated or minimised with modern drugs. Appropriate anti-inflammatory painkillers, for example, can give an arthritic cat a new lease of life.

Symptoms of ill health in elderly cats

Some of the problems that we assume are just caused by getting old are actually symptoms of an unrelated problem that needs treating. For example, experiments in which cats of all ages were taught to walk along a balance beam showed that a loss of balance is not a normal part of aging for a cat. Only a qualified vet has the knowledge and facilities to ensure that your cat's problem is treated appropriately and to advise you on the likely outcome of any treatment plan. So if your cat seems a bit less steady on his feet, or starts limping or is generally off-colour, don't just put it down to old age. Take him to the vets for a check-up.

Spotting the signs of impending problems early is the best way to be able to tackle them, and increases your chances of helping your senior cat to stay healthy for longer. In addition to weight loss, excessive thirst or drinking more than normal, diarrhoea, vomiting and poor appetite are all signs that things are not right. It's a great idea to take your senior cat for regular check-ups, and it's recommended that from middle age cats should have vet checks every six months. As owners it's hard to notice subtle changes in our pets, after all, we see them every day! But these are the things that take on increased significance later in your cat's life. So jot down anything you think might be significant or anything out of the ordinary before you go, together with any questions you want to ask your vet.

Behavioural changes in elderly cats

Studies differ on whether elderly cats suffer serious mental decline, but many owners believe that ageing cats may have sleep and elimination problems, make more noise and even have navigation issues that they didn't have when they were younger. If you are worried about your senior cat getting lost you may be reassured to know that older cats performed just as well as younger cats in spatial learning tests.

Advancing years shouldn't affect your cat's ability to balance.

Some changes in behaviour are understandable and are reflected in our human world. You may notice a slowing down, a lowering of energy and changes in the sleep patterns in your ageing cat. Elderly cats can be more susceptible to stressors, making it even more important to maintain their normal routine, and keep things as calm and cat-friendly as possible around the home. An ageing cat may also experience changes in their relationships with other cats, or become less tolerant of the younger human members of the family. If you think that your cat is behaving differently, your first port of call again should be the vet. It's important not to assume that a major decline in health is inevitable. Issues such as incontinence can often be improved with drugs. And your vet will be able identify any medical issues, prescribe treatment where appropriate, and advise you on caring for your old friend.

Feeding a senior cat

Many senior cats find it more difficult to digest the fat and/or protein in their food as they age. This makes it harder for them to retain body weight and condition, even if they are consuming as much food as they were before. It's also not uncommon for elderly animals to have less appetite, partly because sense of smell and taste declines with age.

If your cat is thriving on the same food he has always had, then there is no need to rush to make a change. If your cat still enjoys his current food, but is losing weight, you can try feeding more of the same. Be aware that many senior cats won't take you up on this kind offer if you just add more to the bowl. Warming food up a little can encourage a cat to eat. Or try offering an extra meal at a different time of the day. Do make sure you increase quantities gradually – 10 per cent at a time is plenty. Overloading a senior digestive system with large quantities of food can end in upset tummies.

However, if your vet has advised that his weight loss might be due to ageing, swapping to a higher protein, higher fat senior cat food could be beneficial. An alternative is to choose a different food that your cat prefers and will eat more of. Easier to digest formulas might help too, and those that are high in energy.

Dietary changes should be made gradually. Unless your vet advises it, don't just switch without warning. Instead mix a little more of the new food with the old each day. This helps to avoid upset stomachs and food refusal, and make the transition smoother for everyone.

Remember, if your elderly cat is on the skinny side, do get them checked up by a veterinary surgeon before making any decisions about their diet. In some cases weight loss can accompany serious health problems such as cancer or kidney disease.

Keeping old cats happy

We can help to keep our elderly cats happy by taking extra care over those daily needs. Part of this means providing for their comfort, and part means monitoring their health a little more closely. Making sure that your cat has easy access to water and the right type of food for his current condition is fundamental. For indoor cats, make sure he can easily climb in and out of his litter box (a ramp can help), and for outdoor cats, check they can still easily work the cat flap. Thin cats may feel the cold and appreciate the luxury of a heated cat bed, or at least a warm rug in a sunny part of the house. Some cats will want to spend more time alone and will need places to have a cosy, secluded nap. Others may want to spend more time in your company.

Make sure your old friend is not struggling with activities such as climbing and jumping. For many years Gadget's preferred means of entry to her home was across a sloping roof and in through a bathroom window left permanently ajar for her. But as she reached her late teens, climbing the roof became more of a struggle for her and the family closed the window and taught her to use the door instead.

Sadly, no matter how well you care for you old friend, there comes a time in all our lives when we have to make the difficult decision to let them go.

Many cats remain youthful well into old age.

Knowing when to let go

With a few adjustments to your life, you and your cat can continue to live together happily even as he starts to wind down. And when he eventually nears the end, you have the power to make sure that his final transition is one that is dignified and fuelled by love. It is all of our dearest hope that when the time comes for our beloved pets they slip gently away in their sleep, preferably at a great age, after having had a nice dinner and a day of cuddles and fun. But very sadly this isn't always how things work out.

Many of our cats in their old age become ill, or lose essential functions like bladder or bowel control, leaving them finding day to day life distressing or uncomfortable. As an owner it's then our responsibility to decide when we think is the right time to let go. And while no one wants to be the person that has to make that decision, we believe that it is fundamentally a good thing that the option is available. There is a saying 'better a week too early than a day too late' and, with very heavy hearts, we have tried to live by this for our pets.

Pets are a massive part of our lives, and missing them is something that we understandably want to put off as long as possible, but we believe that a part of our responsibility to our pets as owners is to put their needs before our own. To make sure that they don't go through weeks of pain or distress with no possible end, just so that we can spend a few more days in their company.

It is common for people to worry that they might be making a difficult choice based on their own convenience. It's tough cleaning up after a sick animal day after day, and natural to want that to end. But being endlessly ill with no hope of recovery is awful for your pet too, so don't feel guilty about bringing your pet's life to an end just because that decision also ends some of your own problems.

The decision to euthanise a beloved pet is obviously still a personal one, and for many of us a caring vet will be a very helpful guide as to when the time has come. It's natural to continue to feel awful once the decision is made. Many people feel guilty for a while too, but this passes with time. Be reassured that modern methods of euthanasia are painless and peaceful. Your cat gave you love, companionship and loyalty. Know that you did the right thing in return by preserving their dignity, and protecting them from pain and distress.

Moving on

There are some very mixed opinions and strong emotions when it comes to the topic of moving on from pet bereavement. How soon, if ever, you feel ready to bring a new cat into your life will vary hugely from person to person, and there are a few things to consider when you decide to make this step.

It's natural to worry that you are replacing your previous pet, but in reality this just isn't the case. Every cat is an individual, unique character. Bringing a new kitten or rescue cat into your home does not mean your old treasured cat is forgotten.

Speak honestly with all of the members of the family and let them express their feelings without judgement. Everyone needs to be on board when it comes to a new pet, even if there is now a cat-sized void in all your lives. It will also mean a period of adjustment, just as when your old cat arrived in your home. Going back to the start, setting up a safe room and gradually becoming comfortable with one another.

The important thing to remember is that your old cat will remain a part of the family, living on in your memories, photos and videos, having provided a hugely worthwhile chapter to all of your lives.

21
Pedigree Cats

edigree cats are a popular choice with some pet parents, and it's no surprise. When you purchase a pure-bred cat you often have a better idea of what to expect in terms of personality, appearance and health. Pure-breeding gives the cat breeder and their customers a predictable outcome. But it does have its downside too. The words pedigree and pure-bred are often used interchangeably, and you'll find more detail on the pros and cons of being pure-bred in Chapter 5: Different Types of Cat. In this chapter we focus on a number of individual pedigree cat breeds and find out whether or not they make great family pets.

We'll give you a brief overview of their personality, special care requirements and any potential health problems to look out for. This information is not exhaustive. As you can imagine entire books have been written solely on each one of these fancy felines. This is a sample of a few breeds that are either popular or unusual, and represents a cross-section of the variety of cat breeds available.

Persian

Due to their iconic appearance and often gentle nature, Persian cats are a popular breed. Although perhaps less playful than some other cats, they are known for also being less predatory – which is a great thing if you like a cat that is a little more chilled out and less likely to harass the hamster! A confident breed, the pretty Persian is also associated with having relatively less fear-based aggression than other cats. It's not just their personality that shines. Persian cats have huge eyes and glossy long coats that usually require regular grooming.

Unfortunately the Persian cat's striking appearance hides some serious health problems. That distinctive flattened face is caused by having what is known as a brachycephalic skull. This means that it is broader and shorter than the average cat's head. Brachycephalic cats are more likely to have breathing problems, overcrowded teeth, blocked tear ducts and poor eye health. Their mouth issues may sometimes require a specialist diet too.

The list of potential Persian problems isn't restricted to those caused by their skull shape. They are prone to heart conditions, liver problems, back problems and polycystic kidney disease (PKD).

If you are considering a Persian kitten then please do research brachycephaly and its consequences first. If you decide to go ahead, look for parents with longer than average muzzles, wider than average nostrils and no tear staining on their face. And do check that the breeder has carried out all the necessary health tests on your kitten's parents, including PKD and PRA (Progressive retinal atrophy) clear certificates for both of them.

Exotic Shorthair

The Exotic Shorthair cat is similar to the Persian. The breed was originally created by outcrossing Persian to American Shorthair cats. They are known for being easy going and affectionate lap cats, although perhaps a little livelier than their Persian predecessors.

Aside from being short rather than long haired, these endearing cats have the exact same breed standard in the Cat Fanciers' Association as the Persian breed does, which unfortunately means that they are also brachycephalic. You will therefore be more likely to have a pet with breathing, eye and teeth problems. In addition to this, polycystic kidney disease is rife in Exotic Shorthairs, with estimates of almost 40 per cent being affected. This condition can sadly result in renal failure from just two years of age. These cats are also prone to urinary problems, with males at a higher risk than females.

Just as with the Persian cat, picking more moderate parents is highly advisable here. Make sure the breeder has fully health tested them both, including a PKD clear certificate and evidence of a vet check.

The Maine Coon is one of the largest breeds of domesticated cat.

Maine Coon

Another very popular breed right now is the magnificent Maine Coon. They aren't just popular for their looks, these cats have bags of character. They have a relatively high prey drive and if kept as indoor pets will need plenty of entertainment. There is also some evidence that Maine Coons may have a slightly greater tendency to be aggressive towards their owners on occasions than other breeds. On the flip side you will find that these cats are less prone to separation anxiety, and are less pushy and attention seeking around the house. They have also been shown in one study to be less likely to mess in the house, which is a bonus we can all appreciate!

The Maine Coon is the biggest domestic breed. There are oodles of social media feeds dedicated to celebrating and showing off the sheer size of these felines with their striking tufted ears and broad muzzles. They can weigh anywhere up to nearly 11 kilograms (24 pounds), but this doesn't mean it's okay for them to be overweight for their build. In fact, in some ways it's even more important to keep them trim – and this is due to the potential for a few genetic diseases.

Heart problems and hip dysplasia are more prevalent in these massive cats than their smaller cousins, but these are both issues that you can help to reduce your cat's chances of getting through carefully searching out breeders that vigilantly health test. There is a genetic link in both cases, and choosing your kittens' parents carefully is half the battle. The other half lies in keeping your Maine Coon slim, fit and healthy. Food allergies may be more likely with these cats, as could be some forms of gastrointestinal trouble. They are relatively more prone to a form of anaemia and reproductive problems.

Just like the Persian, Maine Coon cats have long coats that may require grooming. However, if you get your cat used to being groomed a few times a week from kittenhood, this shouldn't cause too many issues and can even be a nice way to bond. Maine Coon cats come in a spectacular range of colours, from tabby to tortoiseshell, plain or patterned. Interestingly, they are also more likely to have extra toes than other cats! If your Maine Coon seems to have enormous feet even for their size, give their toes a count. You might just be surprised.

When buying a Maine Coon kitten, make sure that both parents have good hip scores and have had a recent vet check confirming no evidence of heart problems.

Siamese cats can be quite vocal.

Siamese

Siamese cats are a unique looking breed, and fairly unique sounding too! Their classic creamy fur is offset with a striking coloured mask, ears, legs and tail. There are several different options when it comes to these coloured extremities or 'points', with seal point and chocolate point being very popular. Siamese cats are always lithe and slender, with startling blue eyes. But some modern lines, known as wedgeheads, have become exaggerated with astounding triangular faces and huge ears.

This is a chatty breed, keen to vocalise their thoughts and feelings throughout the day. Siamese are packed with personality, and although perhaps less sociable than some other breeds they can still bond, and enjoy playtime, with their families.

Unfortunately, these gorgeous kitties have some health issues you will need to be aware of too. There are tests available for some of these problems, progressive retinal atrophy (PRA) for example. This cause of blindness has a genetic link, and if you buy a kitten from two clear parents, your kitten will never show signs of the disease himself. Congenital glaucoma can also be inherited. Other problems are an increased risk of respiratory problems such as feline asthma, and reproductive, urinary and renal problems. Siamese are over represented when it comes to gastrointestinal problems too, from intestinal tumours to mega-oesophagus and pancreatitis.

When buying a kitten make sure that there is no family history of these conditions, and that the parents are DNA tested clear for PRA. Sadly one study showed that this was one of two breeds with the highest mortality under ten years of age. Another breed falling into this unfortunate group was the gorgeous Ragdoll.

Ragdoll

The Ragdoll cat is known for their seriously laid-back attitude, but they can also be quite playful. They are famed for their love of companionship, and are best suited to homes where there is someone around for much of the day. The term Ragdoll came from their tendency to go floppy when picked up, although this isn't a trait that can be guaranteed. A chilled Ragdoll cat may be less likely to jump onto your units or climb your curtains than some other breeds, but their long fur will require regular care and attention.

Heart problems are a potential issue with Ragdoll cats, including a form of hypertrophic cardiomyopathy (HCM) unique to their breed. Males are at a higher risk than females, but regardless of gender it is important to pick a kitten from health-tested parents, with no family history of heart problems.

The Ragdoll is a friendly and affectionate breed.

Potential Ragdoll owners should be aware of the increased risks of gastrointestinal problems, and renal and urinary conditions too. These cats are at a higher risk of having mast cell tumours, a form of cancer, from around the age of 11 years.

Bengal

With their exotic coats and feral-looking build, Bengal cats are truly striking. At first glance they look just like a wildcat, and that's because they were originally bred by mixing domestic cats with the Asian leopard cat. Like the Siamese, the Bengal is a fairly chatty cat with a slightly unusual miaow – sometimes it's compared to a coo or even a chirp! Although Bengal cats are now truly domesticated, they do tend to be on the lively end of the spectrum. If you are keeping a Bengal cat indoors you will need to dedicate plenty of time to daily play sessions. The Bengal loves anything that ticks those predator boxes and works their wild reflexes.

Like many other breeds, cataracts, PRA blindness, urinary conditions and reproductive problems crop up from time to time in the Bengal cat. Fortunately, most risks of the Bengal's health issues can be reduced through health testing. Do make sure both parents are healthy and PRA tested.

Abyssinian

Despite the lack of patterning in the coat, Abyssinian cats are elegant and wild in appearance. With hints of the jungle and a graceful sweep to their bodies, they are known for being exceptionally curious and agile. They are often sociable with people, although perhaps more than averagely averse to other cats.

Reproductive tract difficulties such as uterine infections are a risk in female Abyssinians. PRA is also a common problem in this breed, but avoidable through health screening of the parents before mating.

Abyssinians are prone to renal amyloidosis, which is a condition that causes loss of kidney function. They are also vastly more likely to suffer from loose kneecaps. In fact, one study found that nearly 40 per cent of Abyssinians had knee caps that could be manually dislocated upon applying pressure! Ouch!

The Bengal cat has a striking coat that hints at its wildcat relations.

Sphynx

Is there anything as head-turning as a Sphynx cat? Their bald skin gives them an almost alien look, which is as gorgeous to some as it is shocking to others. But whatever your take, there are a few things you really need to know about the Sphynx.

Cats are meant to have fur – short neat coats that are easy to maintain and keep them warm. But while domestic cats have been bred with a variety of fur types, none is so extreme as the hairless Sphynx. Caused by a genetic anomaly, the problems experienced by the Sphynx cat demonstrate that the purpose of fur is to provide more than just warmth and camouflage. It is also there to protect against bumps and scrapes. And like many genetic mutations, the Sphynx gene is associated with extra problems too – in this case some painful skin conditions, and the prevalence of a progressive muscle disease that causes weak muscles and problems with movement and can give the cat an appearance of being clumsy. Heart and urinary problems are also fairly prevalent in this breed. For all these reasons, if you are considering adding a Sphynx to your family, we urge you to consider adopting an adult cat rather than adding to the demand for these kittens.

Scottish Fold

The Scottish Fold is another distinctive cat, with wide eyes and sometimes unique folded ears. Scottish Folds are all born with upright ears, with folds appearing in some at a few weeks old. The breed can have this expressed as a full fold, or a partial one, or no fold at all. They have short dense coats and large, generously spaced eyes. Their personalities are generally pretty great, with a healthy dash of intelligence and a love of fun and games. But before you go leaping headfirst for this cutie, let's dig a little deeper.

Scottish Folds are possibly one of the most controversial cat breeds, due to the serious health problems caused by the gene responsible for those cute folded ears. The folded ear tips in this breed are the result of a genetic mutation that affects that cat's cartilage. The extent of the fold depends on the cat's genetic make-up, and the ear type you see on the outside reflects to some extent the seriousness of the changes on the inside of affected cats.

The condition Scottish Folds can suffer from is called osteochondrodysplasia. This literally means a failure of normal development of the bone and cartilage. It causes the cartilage in the ears to be soft, hence the fold. But cartilage plays a key role in joints too. Osteochondrodysplasia causes their joints to degenerate, resulting in limited and painful movements, and potentially ending in the joints fusing and the cat becoming far less mobile. The outcome is a playful cat that can't play. The severity and onset of these issues seems to vary from cat to cat. The condition is not curable, though there are ways vets can try to slow the progress and offer pain relief.

Mating two Scottish Folds with fully folded ears is frowned upon as, although it produces only folded kittens, these kittens would all suffer from horrendous joint problems. So most matings are between a folded cat and one that is not folded. But even then problems can occur. If you get lucky and your cat doesn't have trouble with their movement, those tipped ears will still need a lot of maintenance. Just like with floppy-eared dogs, you will need to regularly check and clean them to ensure they don't become infected.

The Scottish Fold also suffers from a raised risk of polycystic kidney disease and heart problems. But their major issue is the joint problems, and these are so serious that we strongly feel that this is a breed best avoided when you are searching for a kitten to join your family.

The world of pedigree cats

There are many more breeds of pedigree cat to choose from. In this section we've reviewed a sample to give you an idea of the range of types and some of the problems that you need to be looking out for. Pedigree cats are not yet as common as pedigree dogs, and many people will be happy with a rescue moggy or kitten from a neighbour. But if you have your heart set on a cat with a particular appearance or temperament, then a pedigree breed may be the way for you to go.

If you are thinking of buying a pedigree cat you will need to do your research to minimise the risk of problems in a breed. The information above is just a starting point. To give your cat the best chance of a healthy life, avoid flat-faced and short-legged breeds, research your new kitten's parents properly, and find a reputable breeder who has done their very best to improve your kitten's chances of avoiding problems. And remember, mixed-breed cats make wonderful pets too.

Ultimately, what we all want from a cat is a happy, contented companion. One that will share our lives for many years to come. And focusing on health is your best chance of achieving that outcome and finding the perfect family cat.

22
Your Happy Cats

We hope that you and your cat are as happy together as we are with our feline family members. Oscar and Billy have brought a huge amount of joy to our lives, and although there have been some bumps along the road, they have all been worth it.

It's important to any cat owner to feel that their pet is as happy with his living situation as they are. So in this final chapter we are going to take a look at spotting those heart-warming signs of contentment in our cats. We will also take a look at whether it would be a good idea to extend your family and add a furry brother or sister into the mix.

Is my cat happy?

Once your cat is settled in as a part of the family, it's natural to want reassurance that he is enjoying the experience as much as you are. A happy cat will be eating well, sleeping well and won't be bothered by normal household sounds and activities. He will be friendly with close members of the family, and able to relax and rest in their company.

When it comes to Lucy's cat Oscar, at nearly seven years old, the family are pretty confident that he is one contented cat. When he walks around his tail stands high. He bumps his head against everyone he meets, strangers included. And even though he isn't a traditional lap cat, he is certainly a next-to-your-lap cat – enjoying joining the family on the sofa in the evening, and slowly blinking his approval when he's looked at. When he was injured by another cat a year or so ago, Lucy had neighbours she had never met asking after him in the street. They told her all about how he came to visit their houses, and even play with their own cats.

Billy is a more reserved character, not one for rushing out to greet the postman, but he offers plenty of affection to his closest friends and carries himself with a similar confident air. He likes to spend winter evenings snuggled up with family members by the fire, but when the weather is fine he likes to be out and about, watching village life from the safety of the garage roof or stalking mice in the hedgerows.

Every cat is different but if your cat greets you with purrs and head bumps, enjoys relaxing at home, indoors or out, and returns regularly for meals and a chat, you can be pretty sure that he too is happy.

Alfie comes to call for Oscar.

Should I get a second cat?

When Billy was about five months old, Pippa seriously toyed with the idea of getting a second kitten or young cat. The joy he brought was so immense, there would be twice as much joy with two? And wouldn't it be wonderful company for Billy?

Oscar, who was adopted around three months before the next-door neighbour's cat, Alfie, seemed an even more likely candidate for a new house-mate. You'd think there would be a few scraps between these neighbouring cats, then some invisible territorial lines would be drawn in the sand outside. But quite the opposite is true. Oscar and Alfie can only be described as friends. They go in and out of each other's houses. When they meet they have been known to walk up to each other and bump heads. They will play gently in the driveway, and even share their food. They actively seek out each other's company.

We both spent quite a while researching the whole issue of multiple cat households, and in the end decided that, on balance, Billy and Oscar might not benefit from a cat friend in the house after all. What follows is how we came to that decision. We started by looking at research into feral cats.

Do cats need friends to be happy?

Feral cats often live in colonies, where they become familiar with each other and can even behave affectionately, just like Oscar and his neighbourhood pal Alfie. Like any other clique, this cat group can be reluctant to add new members into the mix. Although new members may be admitted, this will usually be a drawn-out process lasting several weeks. The research on cat colonies focuses largely on outdoor cats. These are cats who have the choice of interacting with each other or retreating to their own secluded homes or sheltered sleeping places. When you look at cats sharing their accommodation within human houses, things can be rather different. Especially if those cats are indoor only cats.

One study showed that over 44 per cent of multiple cat households had to interrupt at least one cat fight every month. Half of homes find that they are suddenly having to deal with scratching and biting after a new cat is brought into the mix. And when cats do fight, it can be very distressing for you as an owner as well as for the cats involved. It is also thought that in most multi-cat households the aggression tends to go in just one direction, with one cat bullying the other.

Many cats prefer human company to that of other cats.

Your feelings for a cat that regularly beats up the friend you provided for him may change. And cats fighting with each other at home is a major reason for abandonment at rescue centres. But what about the 56 per cent of households where there were no monthly punch ups. That's a good sign right?

Here's the thing. Cats don't always physically fight when they are unhappy. The signs of stress or depression in cats can be very subtle. Excessive washing, miaowing, scratching or shaking of the head can all be indicators that something is not quite right in a multi-cat house. Even when fighting is not taking place, there is evidence that cats living in multiple cat households suffer *constant* levels of stress.

Stress in multiple cat households

Sometimes, raising two kittens together can work out. And you quite possibly know someone who has raised two brother or sisters, or kept a kitten with its mother successfully. But in the long term this arrangement can sometimes go wrong. You may find that the cats seem perfectly happy together when they are young, but then when they reach maturity tensions emerge.

Whether cats fall out as they mature or never got along to begin with, the problems that arise, even in the absence of fighting, can make cats ill. Just like it can with us! From vomiting and diarrhoea to extreme tiredness and a reduction in appetite, these are all linked to cats feeling miserable. There is a strong link between idiopathic cystitis in cats and stress. And cats that live in groups are more likely to suffer from cystitis.

With Oscar and Billy in mind, we both concluded sadly that, while cats do need friends, it seems that in general they need those friends to be humans rather than other cats. There was a significant risk that bringing another cat into either of our homes would diminish Oscar and Billy's quality of life.

'Well that's all very well,' you cry, 'but I've already got two cats and I am determined to make it work!' Fortunately, there are ways to improve the situation for cats that already live in multiple households. It's mostly about providing each cat with sufficient personal space.

How to make multiple cat households work

To keep cats as happy as they can be in the same home it's essential to have enough resources to go around. They shouldn't feel that there is a limit on places to sleep, eat or even poop, and they should feel that if they need some space from each other there is plenty to be found.

Where fights are already breaking out, you can potentially help by more carefully separating these spaces, ensuring that each cat has somewhere that they alone are allowed to go. You might worry that this will make the cats less likely to bond, due to the limited amount of time that they are choosing to spend together, but cats are not like people. Remember how we talked about cats being more likely to seek out affection from their human companions if they were allowed to make the running? Giving the cats the ability to control the terms of their relationships with others can work out a win – win situation for all parties concerned. If your cats willingly start sharing their resources, such as food, water and sleeping spaces, these are good signs that your cats are starting to get along together.

When cats don't get on

If it is not possible to create separate zones and your cats are fighting, or one is being permanently bullied and living in fear, then the bottom line is you will need to consider separating the cats on a permanent basis. This is a choice that no pet owner ever wants to have to make. Bringing home a wonderful new kitten and then having to make the heartbreaking decision to hand them over to a rescue shelter is a terrible thought, but in extreme circumstances it can be the best option for both cats.

This is a big part of the reason that we decided to keep Oscar and Billy as single cats in their own homes. Much as we both would have adored a second cat, we just weren't prepared to take the risk of making our boys miserable. None of this means you shouldn't get another cat, of course. Every home situation is different. Billy and Oscar were destined for life as outdoor cats. They interact with other cats in the village if they choose to. They also get a massive amount of exercise climbing trees, jumping on and off fences and garage rooftops, and chasing mice around the countryside. We both work from home a great deal so they are never bored or lonely.

The situation for an indoor cat may be very different and you need to make your decision based on your own circumstances. If you have your heart set on bringing home a second cat and trying to make it work, then read through the instructions for introducing cats in Chapter 9: Meeting the Family. The key is to create separate zones in your home that each cat can retreat to alone. Introduce the cats slowly and carefully, giving each the opportunity to withdraw. Cat perches in the communal area will help as they allow the cats to observe each other while maintaining physical distance.

If you decide to stick to one cat for now, you are unlikely to regret that decision. Your cat is still very much part of the family, and will be very happy as an only cat, provided you are able to share a few hours with him when he's feeling sociable. Cats quickly figure out when their mealtimes are, and when their family is likely to be about, and adapt their routine accordingly so that you can enjoy time together.

Every kitten has the potential to become the perfect family pet.

The future for cats

Writing *The Happy Cat Handbook* has been an amazing journey for us. We have ploughed our way through hundreds of research papers and clinical trials to try to better understand these extraordinary creatures that share our lives. We've noted some interesting trends and changes in the way that cats fit into our families and society as a whole, especially in the last decade or so. We believe it's likely that ever more cats will be indoor cats in the future, and that we probably need to look at more ways to make life more natural and rewarding for cats that don't have the opportunity to hunt and exercise outdoors. We've also been concerned by some of the changes we have seen with the conformation of our pedigree cat breeds. Cats face similar health problems to dogs when it comes to human interference with their shape and form. We sincerely hope that this won't carry on in future, and that breeders will focus on promoting health over image.

Your family cat

Raising Billy and Oscar is a continuing privilege. In reading this book we hope that you now feel confident in enjoying all of those major milestones in your cat's life – from their arrival as eight-week-old kittens, through the perils of litter box training and those first adventurous steps into the world outdoors, to adulthood.

No book can cover every aspect of cat care in as much depth as we might like, so we have included an extensive resources section for you in the back pages. Whether you want to find out more about diet, entertainment or those troubling health problems, there are studies and books that will help you delve even further into the wonderful world of cats.

A cat is full of contradictions. He is strong and resilient, yet small and vulnerable. At once bold and timid, affectionate and aloof. Cats like to keep us guessing, but what we do know now is that some of the old beliefs about cats were very wrong. They don't only love us for our use of a can opener or provision of a warm fireside spot. Modern domestic cats are no longer solitary animals, they form strong and lasting bonds with their human families that bring them as many rewards as they do to us.

Your cat values you more than you know. What other pet can be given the keys to the world and still choose to come home to their human family? Life with a cat is a pleasure, and an honour. And we hope that you and your cat are as happy together as we are with our furry friends.

A cat to come home to is one of life's great pleasures.

Resources and Further Reading

Websites and organisations

International Cat Care https://icatcare.org

Cats Protection (formerly Cats Protection League) www.cats.org.uk

The Cat Group www.thecatgroup.org.uk

CATalyst Council http://catalystcouncil.org

The Cat Fanciers' Association http://cfa.org

Governing Council of the Cat Fancy www.gccfcats.org

American Association of Feline Practitioners www.catvets.com

The Happy Cat Site www.thehappycatsite.com

AVMA (American Veterinary Medical Association) www.avma.org

Codes of practice and welfare documentation

'Code of Practice for the Welfare of Cats' (DEFRA, December 2017) https://assets.publishing.service.gov.uk/government/uploads/system/uploads/attachment_data/file/697941/pb13332-cop-cats-091204.pdf

Nurse, A. and Ryland, D., 'Cats and the Law: A plain English guide' (The Cat Group, 2014) http://www.thecatgroup.org.uk/pdfs/Cats-law-web.pdf

Books

Bradshaw, J.W.S., Casey R.A. and Brown S.L., *The Behaviour of the Domestic Cat* (CABI, 2012)

Hudson, L. and Hamilton, W., *Atlas of Feline Anatomy for Veterinarians* (Teton NewMedia, 2010)

Robinson, R., *Genetics for Cat Breeders* (Pergamon Press, 1991)

Turner, D.C. and Bateson, P., *The Domestic Cat: The Biology of its Behaviour* (Cambridge University Press, 2013)

Articles

Ahl, A.S., 'The role of vibrissae in behavior: A status review.' *Veterinary Research Communications* 10: 1 (1986): 245–68

Åhman, S.E., et al., 'Cutaneous carriage of *Malassezia* species in healthy and seborrhoeic Sphynx cats and a comparison to carriage in Devon Rex cats.' *Journal of Feline Medicine and Surgery* 11: 12 (2009): 970-6

Armbrust, L.J., et al., 'Gastric emptying in cats using foods varying in fiber content and kibble shapes.' *Veterinary Radiology & Ultrasound* 44: 3 (2005)

Baccus, R.C., et al., 'Gonadectomy and high dietary fat but not high dietary carbohydrate induce gains in body weight and fat of domestic cats.' *British Journal of Nutrition* 98: 3 (2007): 641–50

Barrs, V.R., et al., 'Intestinal obstruction by trichobezoars in five cats.' *Journal of Feline Medicine and Surgery 4* (1999): 199–207

Barrs, V.R., et al., 'Prevalence of autosomal dominant polycystic kidney disease in Persian cats and related-breeds in Sydney and Brisbane.' *Australian Veterinary Journal* 79 (2008): 257–9

Behravesh, C.B., et al., 'Human *salmonella* infections linked to contaminated dry dog and cat food, 2006–2008.' *Pediatrics* 126: 3 (2010)

Bennet, P.C., et al., 'Assessment of domestic cat personality, as perceived by 416 owners, suggests six dimensions.' *Behavioural Processes* 141: 3 (2017): 273–83

Bergsma, D.R. and Brown, K.S., 'White fur, blue eyes, and deafness in the domestic cat.' *Journal of Heredity* 62: 3 (1971): 171–83

Beynen, A.C., et al., 'Clinical signs of hairballs in cats fed a diet enriched with cellulose.' *American Journal of Animal and Veterinary Sciences* 6: 2 (2011): 69–72

Blocker, T. and Van Der Woerdt, A., 'A comparison of corneal sensitivity between brachycephalic and Domestic Short-haired cats.' *Veterinary Ophthalmology* 4: 2 (2001): 127–30

Bonner, S.E., et al., 'Orofacial manifestations of high-rise syndrome in cats: a retrospective study of 84 cases.' *Journal of Veterinary Dentistry* 29 (2012): 10–18

Bowersox, S.S., et al., 'Sleep-wakefulness patterns in the aged cat.' *Clinical Neurophysiology* 58: 3 (1984): 240–52

Boyce, J.T., et al., 'Familial renal amyloidosis in Abyssinian cats.' *Veterinary Pathology* (1 January 1984)

Bradshaw, J.W.S., et al., 'Food selection by the domestic cat, an obligate carnivore.' *Comparative Biochemistry and Physiology Part A: Physiology* 114: 3 (1996): 205–9

Bradshaw, J.W.S., 'Sociality in cats: A comparative review.' *Journal of Veterinary Behavior: Clinical Applications and Research* 11 (2016): 113–24

Bradshaw, J.W.S., 'The evolutionary basis for the feeding behavior of domestic dogs (*Canis familiaris*) and cats (*Felis catus*). *The Journal of Nutrition* 136: 7 (2006): 1927S–31S

Brunt, J., 'Introduction: It's all about the cat: What, why, and how.' *Topics in Companion Animal Medicine* 25: 4 (2010): 177

Buffington, C.A.T., 'External and internal influences on disease risk in cats.' *Journal of the American Veterinary Medical Association* 220: 7 (2002): 994–1002

Buffington, C.A.T., et al., 'Clinical evaluation of cats with nonobstructive urinary tract diseases.' *Journal of the American Veterinary Medical Association* 210: 1 (1997): 46–50

Buffington, C.A.T., et al., 'Clinical evaluation of multimodal environmental modification (MEMO) in the management of cats with idiopathic cystitis.' *Journal of Feline Medicine and Surgery* 8: 4 (2006): 261–8

Butterwick, R.F., et al., 'A study of obese cats on a calorie-controlled weight reduction programme.' *The Veterinary Record* 134: 15 (1994): 372–7

Cafazzo, S. and Natoli, E., 'The social function of tail up in the domestic cat (*Felis silvestris catus*)' *Behavioural Processes* 80: 1 (2009): 60–6

Cameron, M.E., et al., 'A study of environmental and behavioural factors that may be associated with feline idiopathic cystitis.' *Journal of Small Animal Practice* 45 (2006): 144–7

Campbell, S.S. and Tobler, I., 'Animal sleep: A review of sleep duration across phylogeny.' *Neuroscience & Biobehavioral Reviews* 8: 3 (1984): 269–300

Caney, S., 'Weight loss in the elderly cat: Appetite is fine, and everything looks normal.' *Journal of Feline Medicine and Surgery* 11: 9 (2009): 738–46

Cannon, M., 'Hair balls in cats: A normal nuisance or a sign that something is wrong?' *Journal of Feline Medicine and Surgery* 15: 1 (2012): 21–9

Case, J.B., et al., 'Comparison of surgical variables and pain in cats undergoing ovariohysterectomy, laparoscopic-assisted ovariohysterectomy, and laparoscopic ovariectomy.' *Journal of the American Animal Hospital Association* 51: 1 (2015): 1–7

Casey, R.A., et al., 'Reasons for relinquishment and return of domestic cats (*Felis silvestris catus*) to rescue shelters in the UK.' *Anthrozoös* 22: 4 (2009): 347–58

Cave, N.J., et al., 'A cross-sectional study to compare changes in the prevalence and risk factors for feline obesity between 1993 and 2007 in New Zealand.' *Preventative Veterinary Medicine* 107: 1–2 (2012): 121–33

Cave, N.J., et al., 'Systemic effects of periodontal disease in cats.' *Veterinary Quarterly* 32: 3–4 (2012): 131–44

Chang, W.H., et al., 'Study of thermal effects of ultrasound stimulation on fracture healing.' *Bioelectromagnetics* 23: 4 (2002): 256–63

Chen, L.P., et al., 'The effects of frequency of mechanical vibration on experimental fracture healing.' *Zhonghua Wai Ke Za Zhi (Chinese Journal of Surgery)* 32: 4 (1994): 217–9

Chu, K., et al., 'Population characteristics and neuter status of cats living in households in the United States.' *Journal of the American Veterinary Medical Association* 234: 8 (2009): 1023–30

Chung-Chuan, L., et al., 'Common scale-invariant patterns of sleep–wake transitions across mammalian species.' PNAS 101: 50 (2004): 17545–8

Clark, K., et al., 'Comparison of 3 methods of onychectomy.' *The Canadian Veterinary*

Journal 55: 3 (2014): 255–62

Clarke, D.E. and Cameron, A., 'Relationship between diet, dental calculus and periodontal disease in domestic and feral cats in Australia.' *Australian Veterinary Journal* 76 (2008): 690–3

Colliard, L., et al., 'Prevalence and risk factors of obesity in an urban population of healthy cats.' *Journal of Feline Medicine and Surgery* 11: 2 (2009) : 135–40

Corgozinho, K.B., et al., 'Recurrent pulmonary edema secondary to elongated soft palate in a cat.' *Journal of Feline Medicine and Surgery* 14: 6 (2012): 417–9

Cotton, N. and Dodman, N.H., 'Effect of an odor eliminator on feline litter box behavior.' *Journal of Feline Medicine and Surgery* 9: 1 (2007) 44–50

Courcier, E.A., et al., 'An investigation into the epidemiology of feline obesity in Great Britain: results of a cross-sectional study of 47 companion animal practices.' *The Veterinary Record* 171: 22 (2012): 560

Courcier, E.A., et al., 'Prevalence and risk factors for feline obesity in a first opinion practice in Glasgow, Scotland.' *Journal of Feline Medicine and Surgery* 12: 10 (2010): 746–53

Crémieux, J., et al., 'Development of the air righting reflex in cats visually deprived since birth.' *Experimental Brain Research* 54: 3 (1984): 564–6

Crémieux, J., et al., 'Effects of deprivation of vision and vibrissae on goal-directed locomotion in cats.' *Experimental Brain*

Research 65: 1 (1986): 229–34

Crowell-Davis, S.L., et al., 'Social organization in the cat: A modern understanding.' *Journal of Feline Medicine and Surgery* 6: 1 (2004): 19–28

Curtis, T.M., et al., 'Influence of familiarity and relatedness on proximity and allogrooming in domestic cats (*Felis catus*).' *American Journal of Veterinary Research* 64: 9 (2003): 1151–4

Cvejic, D., et al., 'Unilateral and bilateral congenital sensorineural deafness in client-owned pure-breed white cats.' *Journal of Veterinary Internal Medicine* 23: 2 (2009)

Dann, J.R, et al., 'A potential nutritional prophylactic for the reduction of feline hairball symptoms.' *The Journal of Nutrition* 134: 8 (2004): 2124S–5S

Dards, J.L., 'The behaviour of dockyard cats: Interactions of adult males.' *Applied Animal Behaviour Science* 10: 1–2 (1983): 133–53

Day, M.J., 2010. 'Ageing, immunosenescence and inflammageing in the dog and cat.' *Journal of Comparative Pathology* 142: 1 (2010): S60–9

de Meer, G., et al., 'Presence and timing of cat ownership by age 18 and the effect on atopy and asthma at age 28.' *Journal of Allergy and Clinical Immunology* 113: 3 (2004): 433–8

Defauw, P.A.M., et al., 'Risk factors and clinical presentation of cats with feline idiopathic cystitis.' *Journal of Feline Medicine and Surgery* 13: 12 (2011): 967–75

Science 173 (2015): 60–7

Dehasse, J., 'Feline urine spraying.' *Applied Animal Behaviour Science* 52: 3–4 (1997): 365–71

Delgado, M.M., et al., 'Human perceptions of coat color as an indicator of domestic cat personality.' *Anthrozoös* 25: 4 (2012)

Diehl, K., 'Feline gingivitis-stomatitis-pharyngitis.' *Veterinary Clinics: Small Animal Practice* 23: 1 (1993): 139–53

Dinis, F.A.B.S.G., et al., 'Does cat attachment have an effect on human health? A comparison between owners and volunteers.' *Pet Behaviour Science* 1 (2016): 1–12

Donoghue, S. and Scarlett, J.M., 'Diet and feline obesity.' *The Journal of Nutrition* 128: 12 (1998): 2776S–8S

Eckstein, R.A. and Hart, B.L., 'The organization and control of grooming in cats.' *Applied Animal Behaviour Science* 68: 2 (2000): 131–40

Egenvall, A., et al., 'Mortality of life-insured Swedish cats during 1999–2006: Age, breed, sex, and diagnosis.' *Journal of Veterinary Internal Medicine* 23: 6 (2009)

Ekstrand, C. and Linde-Forsberg, C., 'Dystocia in the cat: A retrospective study of 155 cases.' *Journal of Small Animal Practice* 35: 9 (1994)

Ellis, J, et al., 'Does previous use affect litter box appeal in multi-cat households?' *Behavioural Processes* 141: 3 (2017): 284–90

Ellis, S.L.H., et al., 'The influence of body region, handler familiarity and order of region handled on the domestic cat's response to being stroked.' *Applied Animal Behaviour*

Ellis, S.L.H. and Wells, D.L., 'The influence of olfactory stimulation on the behaviour of cats housed in a rescue shelter.' *Applied Animal Behaviour Science* 123: 1–2 (2010): 56–62

Engvall, E. and Bushnell, N., 'Patellar luxation in Abyssinian cats.' *Feline Practice* 19:4 (1990): 20–2

Fabre, M., et al., 'Testing visually guided forepaw movements in the cat: Training apparatus and procedure.' *Physiology & Behaviour* 23: 2 (1979) 263–6

Farrow, H.A., et al., 'Effect of dietary carbohydrate, fat, and protein on postprandial glycemia and energy intake in cats.' *Journal of Veterinary Internal Medicine* 27: 5 (2013)

Fettman, M.J., et al., 'Effects of neutering on bodyweight, metabolic rate and glucose tolerance of domestic cats.' *Research in Veterinary Science* 62: 2 (1997): 131–6

Finlay, R., et al., 'Human health implications of salmonella-contaminated natural pet treats and raw pet food.' *Clinical Infectious Diseases* 42: 5 (2006): 686–91

Flannelly, K.J., et al., 'Vibrissal anesthesia and the suppression of intruder-elicited aggression in rats.' *The Psychological Record* 26: 2 (1976): 255–61

Forrester, S.D., and Towell, T.L., 'Feline idiopathic cystitis.' *Veterinary Clinics: Small Animal Practice* 45: 4 (2015): 783–806

Frank, T., et al., 'The development of the kitten's visual optics.' *Vision Research* 16: 10 (1976): 1145–9

Fraser Sissom, D.E., et al., 'How cats purr.' *Journal of Zoology* 223: 1 (1991)

Friedmann, E. and Thomas, S.A., 'Pet ownership, social support, and one-year survival after acute myocardial infarction in the Cardiac Arrhythmia Suppression Trial (CAST).' *The American Journal of Cardiology* 76: 17 (1995): 1213–17

Gandolfi, B., et al., 'The naked truth: Sphynx and Devon Rex cat breed mutations in *KRT71.' Mammalian Genome* 21: 9–10 (2010): 509–15

Gassel, A.D., et al., 'Comparison of oral and subcutaneous administration of buprenorphine and meloxicam for preemptive analgesia in cats undergoing ovariohysterectomy.' *Journal of the American Veterinary Medical Association* 227: 12 (2005): 1937–44

Gerard, A.F., et al., 'Telephone survey to investigate relationships between onychectomy or onychectomy technique and house soiling in cats.' *Journal of the American Veterinary Medical Association* 249: 6 (2016): 638–43

Ginn, J.A., et al., 'Nasopharyngeal turbinates in brachycephalic dogs and cats.' *Veterinary Clinical Medicine* 44: 5 (2008): 243–9

Goldfinger, M.D. and Fukami, Y., 'Distribution, density and size of muscle receptors in cat tail dorsolateral muscles.' *Journal of Anatomy* 135: 2 (1982): 371–84

Gordon, L.E., et al., 'High-rise syndrome in dogs: 81 cases (1985-1991).' *Journal of the American Veterinary Medical Association* 202: 1 (1993): 118–22

Gourkow, N.G. and Phillips, C.J.C., 'Effect of interactions with humans on behaviour, mucosal immunity and upper respiratory disease of shelter cats rated as contented on arrival.' *Preventative Veterinary Medicine* 121: 3–4 (2015): 288–96

Graf, R., et al., 'Swiss Feline Cancer Registry 1965–2008: the influence of sex, breed and age on tumour types and tumour locations.' *Journal of Comparative Pathology* 154: 2–3 (2016): 195–210

Grant, D.C., 'Effect of water source on intake and urine concentration in healthy cats.' *Journal of Feline Medicine and Surgery* 12: 6 (2010): 431–4

Gunn-Moore, D., et al., 'Breed-related disorders of cats.' *Journal of Small Animal Practice* 49: 4 (2008)

Gunn-Moore, D., et al., 'Cognitive dysfunction and the neurobiology of ageing in cats.' *Journal of Small Animal Practice* 48: 10 (2007)

Gunn-Moore, D.A. and Thrusfield, M.V., 'Feline dystocia: prevalence, and association with cranial conformation and breed.' *The Veterinary Record* 136: 14 (1995): 350–3

Guy, N.C., et al., 'Litterbox size preference in domestic cats (*Felis catus*).' *Journal of Veterinary Behavior: Clinical Applications and Research* 9: 2 (2014): 78–82

Häggström, J., 'Feline cardiomyopathy: Tips and tricks on diagnosis and treatment.'

The Journal of Thai Veterinary Practitioners 24: 3 (2012): 45–9

Hahn, J.F., 'Stimulus–response relationships in first-order sensory fibres from cat vibrissae.' The Journal of Physiology 213: 1 (1971)

Hardie, E.M., et al., 'Radiographic evidence of degenerative joint disease in geriatric cats: 100 cases (1994–1997).' Journal of the American Veterinary Medical Association 220: 5 (2002): 628–32

Harper, E.J., 'Changing perspectives on aging and energy requirements: Aging and digestive function in humans, dogs and cats.' The Journal of Nutrition 128: 12 (1998): 2632S–5S

Hart, B.L., et al., 'Control of urine marking by use of long-term treatment with fluoxetine or clomipramine in cats.' Journal of the American Veterinary Medical Association 226: 3 (2005): 378–82

Hart, B.l., et al., 'Effectiveness of buspirone on urine spraying and inappropriate urination in cats.' Journal of the American Veterinary Medical Association 203: 2 (1993): 254–8

Heath, S. and Wilson, C., 'Canine and feline enrichment in the home and kennel: A guide for practitioners.' Veterinary Clinics: Small Animal Practice 44: 3 (2014): 427–49

Hendrick, M., et al., 'Postvaccinal sarcomas in the cat: epidemiology and electron probe microanalytical identification of aluminum.' Cancer Research 52: 19 (1992): 5391–4

Hendriks, W.H., et al., 'Seasonal hair loss in adult domestic cats (Felis catus).' Journal of

Animal Physiology and Animal Nutrition 79: 2 (1998): 92–101

Herron, M.E., 'Advances in understanding and treatment of feline inappropriate elimination.' Topics in Companion Animal Medicine 25: 4 (2010): 195–202

Horwitz, D.F., 'Behavioral and environmental factors associated with elimination behavior problems in cats: A retrospective study.' Applied Animal Behaviour Science 52: 1–2 (1997): 129–37

Hubler, M., et al., 'Palliative irradiation of Scottish Fold osteochondrodysplasia.' Veterinary Radiology & Ultrasound 45: 6 (2004): 582–5

Jackson, B. and Reed, A., 'Catnip and the alteration of consciousness.' Journal of the American Medical Association 207: 7 (1969): 1349–50

Johns, P.R., et al., 'Postnatal neurogenesis in the kitten retina.' The Journal of Comparative Neurology 187 (1979): 545–5

Kafarnik, C., et al., 'Corneal innervation in mesocephalic and brachycephalic dogs and cats: assessment using in vivo confocal microscopy.' Veterinary Ophthalmology 11: 6 (2008): 363-7

Kane, E., et al., 'Feeding behavior of the cat fed laboratory and commercial diets.' Nutrition Research 1: 5 (1981): 499–507

Keller, G.G., et al., 'Hip dysplasia: A feline population study.' Veterinary Radiology & Ultrasound 40: 5 (1999): 460–4

Kiley-Worthington, M., 'The tail movements of ungulates, canids and felids with particular reference to their causation and function as displays.' *Behaviour* 56: 1 (1976): 69–114

Kirk, C.A., et al., 'Evaluation of factors associated with development of calcium oxalate urolithiasis in cats.' *Journal of the American Veterinary Medical Association* 207: 11 (1995): 1429–34

Kirkwood, P.A., et al., 'Intercostal muscles and purring in the cat: The influence of afferent inputs.' *Brain Research* 405: 1 (1987) 187–91

Kittleson, M.D., et al., 'Familial hypertrophic cardiomyopathy in Maine Coon cats: An animal model of human disease.' *Circulation* 99: 3 (2018): 3172–80

Kral, A. and Lomber, S., 'Deaf white cats.' *Current Biology* 25 (2015) R345–61

Kunzel, W., et al., 'Morphometric investigations of breed-specific features in feline skulls and considerations on their functional implications.' *Anatomia Histologica Embryologia* 32: 4 (2003): 218–23

Kurushima, J., et al., 'Cats of the pharaohs: Genetic comparison of Egyptian cat mummies to their feline contemporaries.' *Journal of Archaeological Science* 39: 10 (2012): 3217–3223

Ladlow, J., 'Injection site-associated sarcoma in the cat: Treatment recommendations and results to date.' *Journal of Feline Medicine and Surgery* 15: 5 (2013): 409–18

Laflamme, D. and Gunn-Moore, D., 'Nutrition of aging cats.' *Veterinary Clinics: Small Animal Practice* 44: 4 (2014): 761–74

Laflamme, D.P., 'Food allergy in dogs and cats.' *Nestle Purina Research Report* 14: 1 (2011)

Laflamme, D.P., 'Nutrition for aging cats and dogs and the importance of body condition.' *Veterinary Clinics: Small Animal Practice* 35: 3 (2005): 713–42

Laflamme, D.P., et al., 'Effect of diets differing in fat content on chronic diarrhea in cats.' *Journal of Veterinary Internal Medicine* 25: 2 (2011)

Laflamme, D.P., et al., 'Pet feeding practices of dog and cat owners in the United States and Australia.' *Journal of the American Veterinary Association* 232: 5 (2008): 687–94

Landsberg, G.M. and Wilson, A.L., 'Effects of clomipramine on cats presented for urine marking.' *Journal of the American Animal Hospital Association* 41: 1 (2005): 3–11

Letitia, M.S., et al., 'Agonistic behavior and environmental enrichment of cats communally housed in a shelter.' *Journal of the American Veterinary Medical Association* 239: 6 (2011): 796–802

Li, X., et al., 'Pseudogenization of a sweet-receptor gene accounts for cats' indifference toward sugar. *PLoS Genetics* 1: 1 (2005)

Linseele, V., et al., 'Evidence for early cat taming in Egypt.' *Journal of Archaeological Science* 34: 12 (2007): 2081–90

Lipinski, M.J., et al., 'The ascent of cat breeds: Genetic evaluations of breeds and worldwide random-bred populations.' *Genomics* 91: 1 (2008): 12–21

Logan, E.I., 'Dietary influence on

periodontal health in dogs and cats.' *Veterinary Clinics: Small Animal Practice* 36 (2006): 1385–1401

Loureiro, B.A., et al., 'Sugarcane fibre may prevents hairball formation in cats.' *Journal of Nutritional Science* 3 (2014)

Lowe, S.E. and Bradshaw, J.W.S., 'Ontogeny of individuality in the domestic cat in the home environment.' *Animal Behaviour* 61: 1 (2001): 231–7

MacDonald, K.A., et al., 'Effect of spironolactone on diastolic function and left ventricular mass in Maine Coon cats with familial hypertrophic cardiomyopathy.' *Journal of Veterinary Internal Medicine* 22: 2 (2008)

Malik, R., et al., 'Osteochondrodysplasia in Scottish Fold cats.' *Australian Veterinary Journal* 77: 2 (2008): 85–92

Martin, P.T., et al., 'Muscular dystrophy associated with α-dystroglycan deficiency in Sphynx and Devon Rex cats.' *Neuromuscular Disorders* 18: 12 (2008): 942–52

McComb, K., et al., 'The cry embedded within the purr.' *Current Biology* 19: 13 (2009): R507–8

McCune, S., 'The impact of paternity and early socialisation on the development of cats' behaviour to people and novel objects.' *Applied Animal Behaviour Science* 45: 1–2 (1995): 109–24

McCune, S., et al., 'Ageing does not significantly affect performance in a spatial learning task in the domestic cat (*Felis silvestris catus*).' *Applied Animal Behaviour Science* 112: 3–4 (2008): 345–56

Megehee, C., 'Can we live without cats? Interpreting and expanding on Ellson's question from a cat-lover's perspective.' *Journal of Business Research* 61: 5 (2008): 574–8

Mertens, C., 'Human-cat interactions in the home setting.' *Anthrozoös* 4: 4 (1991): 214–31

Meurs, K.M., et al., 'A substitution mutation in the myosin binding protein C gene in ragdoll hypertrophic cardiomyopathy.' *Genomics* 90: 2 (2007): 261–4

Moise, N.S., et al., 'Clinical, radiographic, and bronchial cytologic features of cats with bronchial disease: 65 cases (1980–1986).' *Journal of the American Veterinary Medical Association* 194: 10 (1989): 1467–73

Murray, J.K., et al., 'Number and ownership profiles of cats and dogs in the UK.' *Veterinary Record* 166 (2010): 163–8

Murray, J.K., et al., 'Survey of the characteristics of cats owned by households in the UK and factors affecting their neutered status.' *Veterinary Record* 164 (2009): 137–41

Natoli, E., et al., 'Male and female agonistic and affiliative relationships in a social group of farm cats (*Felis catus* L.).' *Behavioural Processes* 53: 1–2 (2001): 137–43

Nibblett, B.M., et al., 'Comparison of stress exhibited by cats examined in a clinic versus a home setting.' *Applied Animal Behaviour Science* 173 (2015): 68–75

Nicastro, N., 'Perceptual and acoustic

evidence for species-level differences in meow vocalizations by domestic cats (*Felis catus*) and African wild cats (*Felis silvestris lybica*).' *Journal of Comparative Psychology* 118: 3 (2004): 287–96

Nilsson, S.F.E., et al., 'Ocular blood flow and retinal metabolism in Abyssinian cats with hereditary retinal degeneration.' *Investigative Ophthalmology and Visual Science* 42: 5 (2001): 1038–44

Ofri, R., et al., ' Characterization of an early-onset, autosomal recessive, progressive retinal degeneration in Bengal cats.' *Investigative Ophthalmology and Visual Science*. 56: 9 (2015): 5299-308

Olson, L.E., et al., 'Review of gunshot injuries in cats and dogs and utility of a triage scoring system to predict short-term outcome: 37 cases (2003–2008).' *Journal of the American Veterinary Medical Association* 245: 8 (2014): 923–9

Overall, K.L., et al., 'Feline behavior guidelines from the American Association of Feline Practitioners.' *Journal of the American Veterinary Medical Association* 227: 1 (2005): 70–84

Oxley, J. and Montrose, T., 'High rise syndrome in cats.' *Vet Times* (24 October 2016)

Pachel, C. and Neilson, J., 'Comparison of feline water consumption between still and flowing water sources: A pilot study.' *Journal of Veterinary Behavior: Clinical Applications and Research* 5: 3 (2010): 130–3

Palen, G.F. and Goddard, G.V., 'Catnip and oestrous behaviour in the cat.' *Animal*

Behaviour 14: 2–3 (1966): 372–7

Payne, J., et al., 'Population characteristics and survival in 127 referred cats with hypertrophic cardiomyopathy (1997 to 2005).' *Journal of Small Animal Practice* 51: 10 (2010)

Peachey, S.E. and Harper, E.J., 'Aging does not influence feeding behavior in cats.' *The Journal of Nutrition* 132: 6 (2002): 1735S–9S

Perzanowski, M.S., et al., 'Effect of cat and dog ownership on sensitization and development of asthma among preteenage children.' *American Journal of Respiratory and Critical Care Medicine* 166: 5 (2002)

Peters, G., 'Purring and similar vocalizations in mammals.' *Mammal Review* 32: 4 (2002): 245–71

Pittari, J., et al., 'American Association of Feline Practitioners: Senior care guidelines.' *Journal of Feline Medicine and Surgery* 11: 9 (2009): 763-78

Pryor, P.A., et al., 'Causes of urine marking in cats and effects of environmental management on frequency of marking.' *Journal of the American Veterinary Medical Association* 219: 12 (2001): 1709–13

Ragen, T.S., et al., 'The ins and outs of the litter box: A detailed ethogram of cat elimination behavior in two contrasting environments.' *Applied Animal Behaviour Science* 194 (2017): 67–78

Rah, H., et al., 'Early-onset, autosomal recessive, progressive retinal atrophy in Persian cats.' *Investigative Ophthalmology and Visual Science* 46: 5 (2005): 1742–7

Randi, E., et al., 'Genetic identification of wild and domestic cats (*Felis silvestris*) and their hybrids using Bayesian clustering methods.' *Molecular Biology and Evolution* 18: 9 (2001): 1679–93

Remmers, J.E. and Gautier, H., 'Neural and mechanical mechanisms of feline purring.' *Respiration Physiology* 16: 3 (1972) 351–61

Rodan, I., 'Understanding feline behavior and application for appropriate handling and management.' *Topics in Companion Animal Medicine* 25: 4 (2010) 178–88

Rodan, I., et al., 'AAFP and ISFM feline-friendly handling guidelines.' *Journal of Feline Medicine and Surgery* 13: 5 (2011): 364–75

Rojas, M.A. and Montenegro, M.A., 'An anatomical and embryological study of the clavicle in cats (*Felis domesticus*) and sheep (*Ovis aries*) during the prenatal period.' *Cells Tissues Organs* 154 (1995): 128–34

Rosenblatt, J.S. and Aronson, L.R., 'The decline of sexual behavior in male cats after castration with special reference to the role of prior sexual experience.' *Behaviour* 12 (1958): 285–338

Saito, A. and Shinozuko, K., 'Vocal recognition of owners by domestic cats (*Felis catus*).' *Animal Cognition* 16: 4 (2013): 685–90

Salman, M.D., et al., 'Behavioral reasons for relinquishment of dogs and cats to 12 shelters.' *Journal of Applied Animal Welfare Science* 3: 2 (2000): 93–106

Schleuter, C., et al., 'Brachycephalic feline noses: CT and anatomical study of the relationship between head conformation and the nasolacrimal drainage system.' *Journal of Feline Medicine and Surgery* 11: 11 (2009): 891–900

Schmidt, P.M., et al., 'Ovarian activity, circulating hormones and sexual behavior in the cat. II. Relationships during pregnancy, parturition, lactation and the postpartum estrus.' *Biology of Reproduction 28*: 3 (1983): 657–71

Schmidt-Künzel, A., et al., 'Tyrosinase and tyrosinase related protein 1 alleles specify domestic cat coat color phenotypes of the albino and brown loci.' *Journal of Heredity* 96: 4 (2005): 289–301

Schwartz, S., 'Separation anxiety syndrome in dogs and cats.' *Journal of the American Veterinary Medical Association* 222: 11 (2003): 1526–32

Scott, D.W. and Paradis, M., 'A survey of canine and feline skin disorders seen in a university practice: Small Animal Clinic, University of Montreal, Saint-Hyacinthe, Québec (1987–1988).' *The Canadian Veterinary Journal* 31 (1990): 830–5

Shipley, C., et al., 'The role of auditory feedback in the vocalizations of cats.' *Experimental Brain Research* 69: 2 (1988): 431–8

Shyan-Norwalt, M., 'Caregiver perceptions of what indoor cats do "for fun".' *Journal of Applied Animal Welfare Science* 8: 3 (2005): 199–209

Smith, A.N., 'The role of neutering in cancer development.' *Veterinary Clinics: Small Animal Practice* 44: 5 (2014): 965–75

Smith, S.A., et al., 'Arterial thromboembolism in cats: Acute crisis in 127 cases (1992–2001) and long-term management with low-dose aspirin in 24 cases.' *Journal of Veterinary Internal Medicine* 17 (2003): 73–83

Soennichsen, S. and Chamove, A.S., 'Responses of cats to petting by humans.' *Anthrozoös* 15: 3 (2002): 258–65

Stammbach, K.B. and Turner, D.C., 'Understanding the human–cat relationship: Human social support or attachment.' *Anthrozoös* 12: 3 (1999): 162-8

Steagall, P.V.M., et al., 'A review of the studies using buprenorphine in cats.' *Journal of Veterinary Internal Medicine* 28: 3 (2014): 762-770

Stella, J., et al., 'Effects of stressors on the behavior and physiology of domestic cats.' *Applied Animal Behaviour Science* 143: 2–4 (2013): 157–63

Stelow, E.A., et al., 'The relationship between coat color and aggressive behaviors in the domestic cat.' *Journal of Applied Animal Welfare Science* 19: 1 (2016): 1–15

Sterman, M.B., et al., 'Circadian sleep and waking patterns in the laboratory cat.' *Clinical Neurophysiology* 19: 5 (1965) 509–17

Strain, G.M., 'The genetics of deafness in domestic animals.' *Frontiers in Veterinary Science* 2 (2015): 29

Szenczi, P., et al., 'Mother–offspring recognition in the domestic cat: Kittens recognize their own mother's call.' *Developmental Psychobiology* 58 (2016): 567–77

Thiess, S., et al., 'Effects of high carbohydrate and high fat diet on plasma metabolite levels and on IV glucose tolerance test in intact and neutered male cats.' *Journal of Feline Medicine and Surgery* 6: 4 (2004): 207–18

Thomas, R.K., 'Vertebrate intelligence: A review of the laboratory research.' In Hoage, R.J. and Goldman, L., eds, *Animal Intelligence: Insights into the Animal Mind* (Smithsonian Institution Press: 1986)

Ticehurst, K., et al., 'Use of continuous positive airway pressure in the acute management of laryngeal paralysis in a cat.' *Australian Veterinary Journal* 86 (2008): 395–7

Todd, N.B., 'Inheritance of the catnip response in domestic cats.' *Journal of Heredity* 53: 2 (1962): 54–6

Torres-Henderson, C., et al., 'Use of Purina Pro Plan Veterinary Diet UR Urinary St/ Ox to dissolve struvite cystoliths.' *Topics in Companion Animal Medicine* 32: 2 (2017): 49–54

Trehiou-Sechi, E., et al., 'Comparative echocardiographic and clinical features of hypertrophic cardiomyopathy in 5 breeds of cats: A retrospective analysis of 344 cases (2001–2011).' *Journal of Veterinary Internal Medicine* 26: 3 (2012) 532–41

Tucker, A.O. and Tucker, S.S., 'Catnip and the catnip response.' *Economic Botany* 42: 2 (1988): 214–31

Turner, D.C., 'A review of over three decades of research on cat-human and human-cat interactions and relationships.' *Behavioural Processes* 141: 3 (2017): 297-304

Tynes. V.V., et al., 'Evaluation of the role of lower urinary tract disease in cats with urine-marking behavior.' *Journal of the American Veterinary Medical Association* 223: 4 (2003): 457-61

Ursin, R., 'Sleep stage relations within the sleep cycles of the cat.' *Brain Research* 11: 2 (1968): 347–56

Van Neer, W., et al., 'More evidence for cat taming at the Predynastic elite cemetery of Hierakonpolis (Upper Egypt).' *Journal of Archaeological Science* 45 (2014): 103–11

Verhaert, L. and Van Wetter, C., 'Survey of oral diseases in cats in Flanders.' *Vlaams Diergeneeskundig Tijdschrift (Flemish Veterinary Journal)* 73 (2004): 331-41

Vnuk, D., et al., 'Feline high-rise syndrome: 119 cases (1998–2001).' *Journal of Feline Medicine and Surgery* 6: 5 (2004): 305–12

Voith, V.L. and Borchelt P.L., 'Elimination behavior problems in cats.' *Readings In Companion Animal Behavior* (Wiley-Blackwell, 1996)

Von Muggenthaler, E., 'The felid purr: A healing mechanism?' *The Journal of the Acoustical Society of America* 110: 2666 (2001)

Walker, C., et al., 1998. Balance in the cat:

Role of the tail and effects of sacrocaudal transection.' *Behavioural Brain Research* 91: 1-2 (1998): 41-7

Wang, S., et al., 'Low intensity ultrasound treatment increases strength in a rat femoral fracture model.' *Journal of Orthopaedic Research* 12: 1 (1994): 40-7

Watson, A.D.J., 'Diet and periodontal disease in dogs and cats.' *Australian Veterinary Journal* 71: 10 (1994): 313–18

Weber, M., et al., 'Influence of the dietary fibre levels on faecal hair excretion after 14 days in short and long-haired domestic cats.' *Veterinary Medicine and Science* 1: 1 (2015): 30-7

Wedl, M., et al., 'Factors influencing the temporal patterns of dyadic behaviours and interactions between domestic cats and their owners.' *Behavioural Processes* 86: 1 (2011): 58–67

Weese, J.S., et al., 'Bacteriological evaluation of commercial canine and feline raw diets.' *The Canadian Veterinary Journal* 46: 6 (2005): 513–16

Whalen, R.E., 'Sexual Behavior of Cats.' *Behaviour* 20: 3 (1963) 321-42

Whitney, W.O. and Mehlhaff, C.J., 'High-rise syndrome in cats.' *Journal of the American Veterinary Association* 191: 11 (1987): 1399–1403

Wilson, C., et al., 'Owner observations regarding cat scratching behavior: An internet-based survey.' *Journal of Feline Medicine and Surgery* 18: 10 (2016): 791-7

Windle, W.F. and Fish, M.W., 'The

development of the vestibular righting reflex in the cat.' *Journal of Comparative Neurology* 54 (1932): 85–96

Yeon, S.C., et al., 'Differences between vocalization evoked by social stimuli in feral cats and house cats.' *Behavioural Processes* 87: 2 (2011) 183–9

Zoran, D.L., 'The carnivore connection to nutrition in cats.' *Journal of the American Veterinary Medical Association* 221: 11 (2002): 1559–67

Zoran, D.L., et al., 'Effects of nutrition choices and lifestyle changes on the well-being of cats, a carnivore that has moved indoors.' *Journal of the American Veterinary Medical Association* 239: 5 (2011): 596–606

Acknowledgements

Thank you so much to everyone who helped bring this book together.

We couldn't have done it without the love and support of our family and friends, and the wonderful team at Christopher Little's agency, especially Chris and Emma. Thanks also to Carey, Samantha and Charlotte from Ebury press.

Special thanks for our husbands, Matt Easton and Duncan Mattinson, for their love and support from start to finish. To Sammie Austwick, for her excellent and honest input on the manuscript. And to Tom Mattinson, Toby Mattinson, Sarah Holloway, Laney Harris and everyone else who listened to our ever-evolving ideas and came along with us for the ride.

And thanks most of all to Oscar and Billy. The furry inspiration for this book, and loving companions that bring warmth and humour to our lives.

Index